Literature Searching
in Science,
Technology,
and Agriculture

Literature Searching in Science, Technology, and Agriculture

EILEEN PRITCHARD
and
PAULA R. SCOTT

GREENWOOD PRESS
Westport, Connecticut • London, England

Library of Congress Cataloging in Publication Data

Pritchard, Eileen.
  Literature searching in science, technology, and
agriculture.

  Includes index.
  1. Information storage and retrieval systems—
Science. 2. Information storage and retrieval systems—
Technology. 3. Information storage and retrieval
systems—Agriculture. I. Scott, Paula R. II. Title.
Z699.5.S3P74 1984   025'.065   83-18471
ISBN 0-313-23710-7 (lib. bdg.)

Library of Congress Catalog Card Number: 83-18471
ISBN: 0-313-23710-7

First published in 1984

Greenwood Press
A division of Congressional Information Service, Inc.
88 Post Road West, Westport, Connecticut 06881

Printed in the United States of America

10 9 8 7 6 5 4 3 2 1

Contents

vi   Contents

Preface

This introduction to library research in science, technology,
and agriculture provides an overview of the most basic
library tools in these areas for college students, library
personnel unfamiliar with scientific materials, and persons
interested in beginning scientific investigation. It stresses
the interdisciplinary nature of investigation in a general
approach to the major abstracting and indexing services and
the most representative reference books, style manuals, and
guides.

The material in this work is arranged to correspond to the
order of procedures in which a person would undertake a
literature search. The contents are both a guide to doing a
literature search and a reference to listings of basic sources
and databases.

Most guides to scientific literature are arranged by subject
and/or by types of literature, and provide lists of many
reference works and detailed descriptions of the types of
literature. Their intent is to be as comprehensive as
possible. The authors found that these guides contained
excessive information for library users seeking a briefer
discussion of important library tools and research techniques.
Other guides had a format corresponding to the sequence of a
literature search, but added material on library operations
which seemed suitable only for librarians, and lacked other
important features (adequate material on database searching
and style manuals). The approach taken here evolved from
classes in scientific literature searching conducted by the
authors at a major academic library. One of the authors
needed material to simplify interpretation of the abstracts
and indexes for her students. Additional information was
added to explain other directions for research as these arose
in class discussions.

The initial chapters orient the reader to types of literature,
search preparation, and finding books in libraries. The
search strategy chapter outlines basic steps of the literature search process, utilizing a number of charts. These

charts lead the searcher from the basic sources to the
specialized; delineate which types of sources to use according to one's need; and recommend procedures according to the
experience of the user.

The abstract and index chapters present the major publications
in a subject sequence, procedures for using them; and access
points or indexes available in each. Additional sections are
devoted to abstracting and indexing services for special
types of literature; i.e., reviews, conference proceedings,
dissertations, and government publications.

Basic logic of computer searching is explained and searches
from different vendors are compared in Chapter 8. Computer
systems and databases included are BRS, SDC, DIALOG, MEDLINE,
and SCISEARCH. Other features of the chapter are lists of
the advantages and disadvantages of doing computer searches
and recommendations for computer search preparation.

No attempt is made to cover all of the important reference
books, since that task has been accomplished in many guides
to scientific literature. Chapter 9 outlines the types of
reference books and lists the appropriate guides to scientific
literature which provide information on reference books.

The chapter "Citing the Literature in a Bibliography" illustrates four basic styles of citation and lists 10 style
manuals used in the scientific disciplines.

Appendices list abstracts and indexes, selected journals,
databases, and sources for review articles.

Acknowledgments

We wish to acknowledge all those who contributed to the
preparation and writing of this book: Angelina Martinez
for her encouragement to write the book, Ted Dawes for his
suggestion to broaden the subject content and submit it for
publication, and Chi Su Kim and Art Antony for their exper-
tise.   We are especially grateful to our typist, Rosemary
Wagner; her ingenuity made the production of the book
possible.

Literature Searching in Science, Technology, and Agriculture

1
Surveying the Types of Literature

There are many different kinds of materials available to the
researcher. In this chapter we will explore briefly the
nature of these resources and their varied formats. The
remaining chapters of this guide will explain how to find
and utilize them. The forms of information may be divided
into primary and secondary sources. Primary sources are
those in which the records of events are first reported or
disseminated. Secondary sources result from analysis,
description, and synthesis of primary sources.

Primary Sources

The Scientific Journal. Modern primary journals contain
articles which are reports of original research or original
observations. The journal article may have evolved from the
paper prepared for oral delivery at meetings of scholarly
societies, or perhaps from prize essays which early societies
developed to stimulate scientific research.[1]

The modern scientific journal article often has a set format.
There may or may not be a summary, or abstract, at the
beginning of the article. There is usually an introduction
which states the problem examined in the article, the
importance of the study, and how it relates to other work in
the field. The introduction is followed by the material and
methods section which outlines the researchers' methodology:
description of the objects of study, test conditions, and
procedures. Next are the results, or observations, which
are the main data of the study and may take the form of
diagrams, photographs, tables, and graphs, in addition to
the narrative. Often this is the longest section. The
discussion brings the results together, evaluates them, and
interprets them in the light of other research. There is

---

[1]"Information processing," Encyclopaedia Britannica,
(15th ed.) IX, 568.

usually a reference section at the end of the article listing
the literature cited in the work.

Trade Journals. Practical information related to persons in
industry is conveyed in the trade journal. The content
includes business news, product information, advertising, and
trade articles. The journals can provide a great deal of
information on current trends in technology, and are useful
to persons seeking orientation to a vocation. Some examples
of trade journals are Aviation Week and Space Technology,
Livestock, Chemical Marketing Reporter, and Professional
Engineer.

The Technical Report. Technical reports are accounts of work
done on research projects; they are written to provide
information to employees and other research workers. A
report may emanate from completed research or on-going
research projects. Private companies and associations use
reports internally for communication within the organization,
and occasionally for public distribution. Governments
support many technical reports by means of grants and
government contracts. Government reports are usually published as separates and may be kept with government documents.
Sometimes the reports appear in series with identifying
report numbers, and the number may be crucial in being able
to locate the desired document. Reports may be confidential
and accessible only to select individuals with security
clearances. National Aeronautics and Space Administration
(NASA) is one of the main producers of technical report
literature. Many technical reports are distributed by the
National Technical Information Service (NTIS). NTIS
strives to make available all unclassified results of
federal research. Its index is the Government Reports
Announcements & Index.

Proceedings. Scientists present original research findings
and review articles at professional meetings. Often these
are published and distributed in various forms. The meetings
may be referred to as symposia, conferences, institutes,
workshops, or colloquia. They provide an important channel
of communication for scientists and an important source of
information for researchers.

Abstracts of Research in Progress. Abstracts may be primary
sources when they are used to report research in progress
presented at a meeting before the journal research article
appears. Many biological meetings are reported on in this
way. For example, the Genetics Society of America issues
abstracts of this kind for their meetings. These abstracts
are often published in the society's journal; note sections
of them in the journal Genetics. Often the initial talk and

associated abstracts are used to test a new interpretation
of results of research.

Dissertations. Doctoral dissertations are another primary
source of scientific publication. In the sciences, the
awarding of a Ph.D. degree usually requires completion of a
major monograph including extensive experimentation, reporting on the results, and suggesting future implications. The
dissertations are kept in libraries at the home schools of
the doctoral candidates and are indexed in Dissertation
Abstracts International. They can be purchased from
University Microfilms International.

Patents. Patents are rights granted by law for the protection of inventions or discoveries. Patent specifications
describe designs, methods and processes of the invention, and
are, therefore, an important source of information for the
engineer, physicist, chemist, and other researchers. To
locate patents there are commercial indexing services such
as Chemical Abstracts which include patents, and government
patent indexes. · The main one for the United States is the
Official Gazette of the United States Patent and Trademark
Office. Recently, database searching has become useful in
examination of patent literature.

Standards. Standards are requirements for the quality or
size or shape of industrial products. They also comprise
recommendations for methods and processes in manufacturing.
Standards are prepared by a variety of trade associations,
national and international bodies. Some types of standards
include quality and measure recommendations, testing
materials, and definitions of trade terms. Some important
groups working on standards in the United States are the
American National Standards Institute (which serves as a
clearinghouse for many types of standards), the American
Society for Testing Materials (which establishes many
standards and develops test methods), and the National
Bureau of Standards (which concerns itself mainly with
physical measurement). The Visual Search Micro Film (VSMF)
service is a good source for retrieval of different
standards.

Secondary Sources

Abstracts. There are many services which abstract and index
technical publications so that researchers can select important papers quickly in their field of interest. The most
important abstracting services are described in later
chapters of this book. Traditionally, abstracts appear
in two forms: the descriptive abstract, which indicates
what is discussed in the original documents, and the
informative abstract, which attempts to present all the
significant data and conclusions of the original document.

In the United States, for example, <u>Chemical Abstracts</u> and
<u>Biological Abstracts</u> provide major abstracting services.

<u>Reviews</u>. Review articles "distill the existing knowledge
relevant to a particular subject into a compact, accessible
form. A typical review article focuses on important advances
which have been made in a specialty, evaluates research,
indicates where gaps in knowledge exist, and provides a
comprehensive bibliography on the subject."[2] The review
article can be the most efficient starting point for a
search of the literature on a particular topic. There are
collections of reviews which are published on an annual
basis by a company called "Annual Reviews, Inc." Many other
publishers are also collecting reviews to cover the state of
the art in specific fields. Titles of review serials are
typically "advances in," "annual review of," "progress in,"
and "yearbook of."

<u>Specialized Books</u>. There are many important books that
contain authoritative information and are considered to be
basic in the field. Students need to make note of these
works, which are sometimes mentioned by instructors or noted
in guides to the literature. Some examples of basic biology
books are--

    Mayr, Ernest. <u>Animal Species and Evolution</u>.
      Cambridge: Belknap Press of Harvard University
      Press, 1963.

    Stebbins, George Ledyard. <u>Variation and Evolution</u>
      <u>In Plants</u>. New York: Columbia University Press,
      1950.

<u>Reference Books</u>. In many cases, specific facts or a summary
of a topic are all that is required. Handbooks, manuals,
encyclopedias, and dictionaries perform this function.
There are also reference materials which refer the inquirer
to other works which will provide the desired information.
A multitude of different reference aids can aid the
researcher (See Chapter 12 on reference sources).

<u>Some Important Sources of Information Which May</u>
<u>Publish Primary or Secondary Source Material</u>

<u>Government Publications</u>. There are many government agencies
publishing works of interest to scientists and technicians.
The United States Department of Agriculture, Smithsonian
Institution, and the United States Department of the Interior
are examples of important agencies which publish many valuable

---

[2] Institute for Scientific Information, <u>The First Place</u>
<u>to Look is the Index to Scientific Reviews</u>. (Philadelphia:
Institute for Scientific Information, [n.d.]), p. 1.

documents.   The format of government publications varies
widely; there are periodicals, monographs, reports, micro-
forms, and others.

Agricultural Experiment Station and Extension Service
Publications.   The state agricultural experiment stations
conduct agricultural research to find answers to problems
common to farmers (and consumers).   There is usually one
station in each state.   The stations publish periodicals,
bulletins, reports, circulars, and miscellaneous publications.
The documents contain valuable research material which is
closely related to the problems of agricultural and food
production.   Related to the experiment stations is the
Cooperative Extension Service, which communicates the
research findings of the stations and the United States
Department of Agriculture to citizens, especially farmers,
through the county and state extension offices.

2
Formulating a Basic Search Strategy

Introduction

In implementing a research project, one must successfully
analyze a question appropriate to the topic and the method
to solve the question. In this chapter, the authors will
discuss (1) how to decide on a research topic, (2) how to
limit a topic, and (3) how to form a search strategy for
obtaining the desired information.

Because of the complexity of information resources, library
research is not easy. It may be frustrating because of the
time required to obtain needed sources. Searching indexes
and abstracts usually takes more time than expected. The
library may have to request materials from other libraries
on interlibrary loan. The information may not correspond to
expectation. These are a few reasons why it is important to
plan a library search carefully, allowing ample time to
complete a project.

Choosing a Topic

Many sources from printed material, radio, and television
may suggest topics for term papers and seminars. Often,
newspaper articles can provide ideas. Papers such as the
New York Times, Wall Street Journal, Christian Science
Monitor, or a local paper may have a report worth pursuing.
One must be careful about choosing articles from newspapers
in which the events are so new that little is available on
the topic elsewhere. Sometimes a newspaper article will
reflect such a simplification of complex research that it is
too difficult to pursue the topic further. Periodicals such
as Newsweek and Time also report scientific discoveries. The
same considerations for newspapers also apply to these publications. Television may be a good source; Nova and other
public television programs often present subjects suitable
for further investigation.

There are several general science magazines for the public
and the general academic audience such as <u>Science 8-</u>,
<u>Discover</u>, <u>Omni</u>, <u>Science Digest</u>, and <u>Science News</u>. They have
eye-catching titles and articles on the latest discoveries.
<u>Science News</u>, a weekly, has articles which are often only
two or three paragraphs of highly condensed explanation.
The other four journals appear monthly and include news and
longer feature articles. The British magazine, <u>New Scientist</u>,
is another general magazine which usually consists of short
articles written by authorities or the <u>New Scientist</u> staff.
This journal is decidedly more political than the above
American counterparts.

Yearbooks to encyclopedias, such as <u>Science Year</u>, have
reports of current happenings and articles of current
interest. These can be helpful in selecting a topic.

<u>Scientific American</u> and <u>American Scientist</u> are two excellent
journals for topics. Articles from <u>Scientific American</u> often
inspire seminar topics, and <u>Scientific American</u> attracts
readers from the general public as well as scientists. This
journal, available on newsstands as well as by subscription,
has contributors who are authorities in their f elds and who
are often well known scientists. <u>Scientific American</u> has
noteworthy illustrations which are often reproduced elsewhere
in books and lectures. For each article, <u>Scientific American</u>
has a short list of references which can be helpful in pursuing the topic further.

The <u>American Scientist</u> discusses topics similar to those in
<u>Scientific American</u>. Although not a newsstand magazine, its
articles are often a little easier to read. The authors,
who are authorities, document their articles well, so it is
easy to find earlier articles on the topics. The references
are sometimes extensive. Sigma Xi, the Scientific Research
Society of North America, publishes this journal for its
members, but it is available in libraries.

The American Association for the Advancement of Science
publishes the weekly journal <u>Science</u>. It covers the broad
spectrum of science and consists primarily of short research
reports. It also includes a few longer articles which
review the literature. Both types of articles have valuable
references to other publications.

<u>Nature</u>, a British journal, serves the same function as
<u>Science</u>. Both <u>Science</u> and <u>Nature</u> can serve as sources of
ideas for the more scientific and specialized papers and
for seminars.

Limiting a Topic

Individual circumstances determine the extent of literature searching. The library user will consider the following:

1. The size of the library's collection on one's chosen subject, and

2. Time limitations for deadlines, interlibrary loans, and library accessibility.

The type of assignment will influence student decisions. To write a short paper, one may wish to limit searching to fewer indexes and use fewer articles. For a seminar, one will search more thoroughly, and a more extensive library collection may be necessary.

In order to get an idea of whether a topic is well covered, it is a good idea to do a preliminary search in an index service. This will reveal whether the topic is:

1. manageable--is there too much or too little on the topic?

2. relevant--does the topic appear in the literature?

3. in a foreign language--is it understandable to the user?

A preliminary search should also include looking at the library's journal holdings to determine the availability of articles.

In determining whether a topic is manageable, the following clues may be of assistance:

1. See if there are more than five citations in a five-year period (usually the last five years) of a Wilson Company index (for titles see page 34); if so, think about narrowing the topic.

2. Probably 15 to 25 citations will be about the right number for the total number of citations for a paper. Much will depend on the nature of the research project.

3. It may help to use a review paper to narrow or limit a topic, because a review paper alerts the reader to what research has been done and what research could be done.

4. In the Permuterm Subject Index of Science Citation Index, a quick perusal of the number of key terms which match a chosen topic may be helpful in determining the amount of material available. Using the five-year cumulations will make the search even easier.

SEARCH STRATEGY FOR THE NOVICE SEARCHER

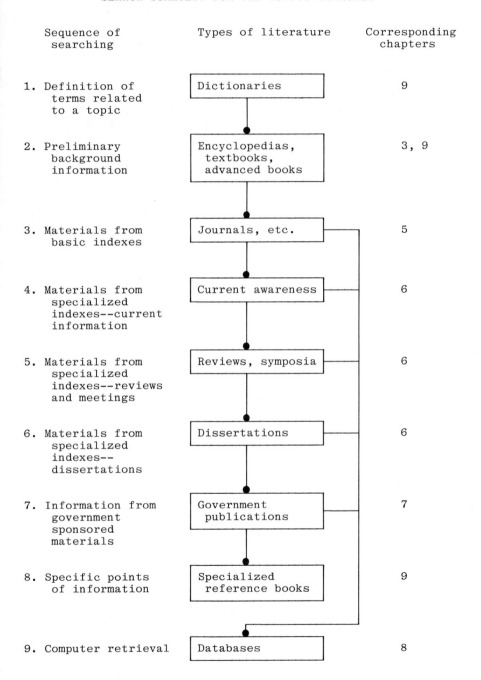

Sequence of searching	Types of literature	Corresponding chapters
1. Definition of terms related to a topic	Dictionaries	9
2. Preliminary background information	Encyclopedias, textbooks, advanced books	3, 9
3. Materials from basic indexes	Journals, etc.	5
4. Materials from specialized indexes--current information	Current awareness	6
5. Materials from specialized indexes--reviews and meetings	Reviews, symposia	6
6. Materials from specialized indexes-- dissertations	Dissertations	6
7. Information from government sponsored materials	Government publications	7
8. Specific points of information	Specialized reference books	9
9. Computer retrieval	Databases	8

STEPS IN SEARCH STRATEGY FOR THE NOVICE SEARCHER

Assignment	1. Dictionaries	2. Encyclopedias	3. Journals	4. Current awareness	5. Reviews, symposia	6. Dissertations	7. Government publications	8. Reference books	9. Databases
Article on topic, beginning student	X	X	X or	X					
Article on topic, advanced student			X or	X					
Short talk, beginning student	X	X	X or	X					
Short talk, advanced student			X or	X					
Term paper, beginning student	X	X	X	X			*	*	
Term paper, advanced student			X	X	X		*	*	*
Seminar, advanced student			X	X	X		*		*
Thesis			X	X	X	X	X	*	X

X should use   * optional, depending on topic

SEARCH STRATEGY FOR THE EXPERIENCED SEARCHER

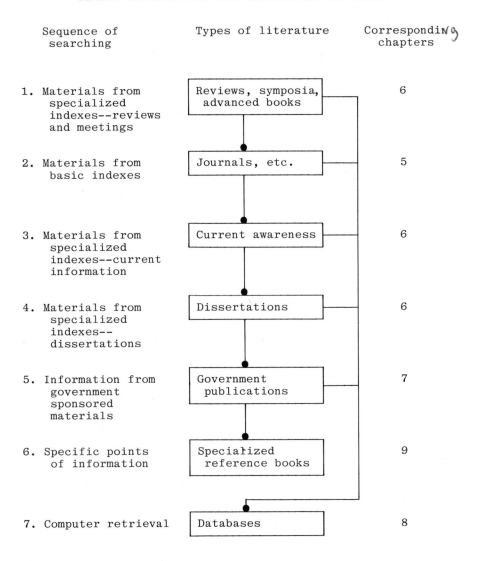

Sequence of searching	Types of literature	Corresponding chapters
1. Materials from specialized indexes--reviews and meetings	Reviews, symposia, advanced books	6
2. Materials from basic indexes	Journals, etc.	5
3. Materials from specialized indexes--current information	Current awareness	6
4. Materials from specialized indexes-- dissertations	Dissertations	6
5. Information from government sponsored materials	Government publications	7
6. Specific points of information	Specialized reference books	9
7. Computer retrieval	Databases	8

STEPS IN THE SEARCH STRATEGY FOR THE EXPERIENCED SEARCHER

Assignment	1. Reviews, symposia	2. Journals	3. Current awareness	4. Dissertations	5. Government publications	6. Reference books	7. Databases
Article on topic advanced student		X or	X				
Short talk advanced student		X or	X				
Term paper advanced student	X	X	X				*
Seminar advanced student	X	X	X		*		*
Thesis	X	X	X	X	X	*	X

X should use   * optional, depending on topic

Search Strategy

1. Definition of terms related to a topic:

   An understanding of the chosen subject is prerequisite
   to searching in bibliographic sources. Dictionaries
   containing scientific and technical terms can clarify
   basic terminology. An example of a dictionary of this
   type is the McGraw-Hill Dictionary of Scientific &
   Technical Terms, McGraw-Hill, 1978. The reference
   departments of academic and large public libraries
   contain more specialized dictionaries for particular
   disciplines. A good dictionary of medical terms, for
   example, is Dorland's Illustrated Medical Dictionary,
   Saunders, 1981.

2. Preliminary background information:

   To gain general background information and to understand
   how a subject relates to the various fields of knowledge,
   an encyclopedia and/or textbook can provide a good introduction to the subject. A comprehensive scientific
   encyclopedia is the McGraw-Hill Encyclopedia of Science &
   Technology, McGraw-Hill, 1977. A textbook may also aid
   in getting a broader perspective of the topic. For
   example, one may begin in a general textbook such as a
   general biology text and progress to a more specific
   text such as one in plant physiology or an advanced book
   on plant hormones.

3. Materials from basic indexes:

   Journal articles provide most of the original research
   information. Indexes and abstracts guide the researcher
   to journal articles, sometimes review articles, and
   symposia. Indexes may also include listings of books,
   reports, or even dissertations. The Bibliography of
   Agriculture indexes United States Department of Agriculture publications, Agricultural Experiment Station and
   Extension Service publications, and Food and Agriculture
   Organization publications, in addition to journals.
   Indexes in engineering, such as the Engineering Index,
   list reports as well as journal articles. The abstracts
   and indexes discussed in Chapter 5 are main sources for
   citations to scientific and technical literature.

4. Materials from specialized indexes--current information:

   Chapter 6 discusses current awareness journals and
   indexes. These are important because they cover materials
   too recent to be indexed in the more comprehensive
   abstracts and indexes discussed in Chapter 5. A good
   paper or thesis should include a search for the most
   current materials.

5. Materials from specialized indexes--reviews and meetings:

    Since the review and symposia papers are not as vital as
    original research in journals, their indexes are placed
    in step 5 of the first search strategy diagram. A more
    experienced searcher may wish to search for reviews and
    symposia first (see Search Strategy for the Experienced
    Searcher).

6. Materials from specialized indexes--dissertations:

    It is probably not necessary to look for dissertations
    when writing a term paper. Dissertations can be useful
    if the topic needs comprehensive coverage. If the
    material is important, it will usually appear in journal
    literature.

7. Information from government materials:

    The United States Government, state governments, and the
    United Nations are examples of publishers of specialized
    governmental materials which may provide information to
    someone writing a paper or doing research. Federal docu-
    ments are especially rich in information in many subject
    areas. Since many branches of the government may study
    aspects of science, technology, or agriculture, it is
    important to search the abstracts and indexes, such as
    those in Chapter 7, to find government publications.
    Government publications are particularly important in the
    field of agriculture. Statistics are also found in
    government publications, since government agencies collect
    many statistics.

8. Specific points of information:

    The library user occasionally needs one fact or statisti-
    cal information derived from a table. Many reference
    books contain short explanations or collections of facts
    and data. Chapter 9 discusses types of reference books
    and where to find more complete lists of reference
    sources.

9. Computer retrieval--databases:

    If the major part of the significant material is within
    the last ten years, the researcher may wish to utilize a
    database search. A database search may save much search-
    ing time in the library. For a short paper, a database
    search is usually unnecessary, but for a longer or more
    thorough paper, a database search is a strong possibility.
    For more information on whether to utilize a database
    search or not, read Chapter 8.

Additional Advice

The authors have found the following guidelines to be useful
in searching:

1. Start a search in the most recent issue of an
   abstract or index.

2. For older editions of an index, look for cumulative
   indexes. Chemical Abstracts, for example, has cumulations of ten years and more recently five years.

3. Look for review articles.

4. It is a good idea to check more than one index to
   see if terms lacking in one may be in another.
   The term "Ene Reaction" is not found in the more
   recent years of Chemical Abstracts, but is found
   in Science Citation Index.

3
Finding Books in a Library

The library user may wish to get a general idea of a subject
in a textbook or reference book before starting research in
other materials. One should locate the collection index
(card catalog) in the library; it is the usual finding
device for books. The physical form taken by the index may
vary; it may be a card catalog, microfilm, microfiche, or
on-line catalog with a cathode ray tube, or a combination of
these.

Card Catalog

Traditionally the form has been a card catalog--cabinets
containing cards for authors, titles and subjects. (See
illustrations on pages 17, 19, and 20.) The cards may be
in one alphabetical sequence or divided; a divided catalog
may have author and title cards in one alphabetical arrangement and subject cards in another.

Microcatalogs

The card catalog is changing format in many libraries. The
wooden cabinets with cards are being replaced by catalogs in
the form of microfiche cards or microfilms which can be
viewed on reading machines. The user may consult a microfilm
catalog by pushing a button to display alphabetically a
desired array of entries on a screen or select a microfiche
card with the appropriate entries also magnified on a screen.
There are varying amounts of information given, depending on
individual library needs: the microcatalog may display all
information normally found in a traditional card catalog; it
may indicate slightly less information, including author,
title, and a bibliographical description of the cataloged
item; or perhaps it displays only the briefest indication of
an item (author, title, and call number). Reasons for the
change to the microform include lack of space for the old
card catalogs, difficulties in maintaining them, and the

technological capabilities for making the new catalogs rapidly from information stored in computer data banks. The microform catalogs are referred to as COM (computer output microform).

On-Line Catalogs

Some libraries provide direct access to library holdings information stored in computer data banks. The library user is able to locate a specific item or browse through the library collection by means of a computer terminal. The call number, title, or author (usually the author and title are abbreviated) is typed at the terminal, and the computer responds with the appropriate data on the terminal display screen. Variations of on-line capabilities allow searching by subject and information about circulation status of library materials. There are also large computer systems which collect data from many libraries and disseminate that data to subscribers. The largest of these is based in Ohio, and is called OCLC (Online Computer Library Center).

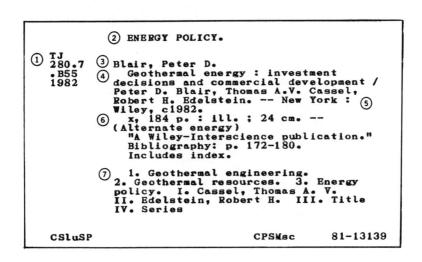

1. Call number. 2. Subject heading. 3. Author. 4. Title. 5. Imprint, or publishing information. 6. Collation, or physical description. 7. Tracings, or indications of other entries in catalog.

Access Points

Books and other library materials may be found in the collection index under different headings: subjects, authors, titles, and series. In a card catalog, cards for subjects have the subject typed on the top of the card in capital letters.

Subject Headings

Most libraries use the Library of Congress Subject Headings as the source of subjects listed in their catalogs. Some specialized libraries may use different subject headings. An excerpt from the Library of Congress Subject Headings in Microform is shown in the following list.

(1) Scientific expeditions (Indirect) (Q115) (2)
   (3) sa names of regions explored, e.g. Africa, Central;
          Antarctic regions; Arctic regions; also names
          of expeditions, e.g. Challenger Expedition,
          1872-1876; and names of ships
   (4) x Expeditions, Scientific
        Polar expeditions
        Scientific voyages
        Travels
        Voyages, Scientific
   (5) xx Antarctic regions
        Arctic regions
        Discoveries (in geography)
        Voyages and travels
   (6) --Equipment and supplies (Q116)
      Scientific French
   (7) See French language--Technical French
      Scientific illustration
          sa Biological illustration
          Drawing--Scientific applications

1. Valid subject heading. 2. Library of Congress class number designation for books about scientific expeditions. 3. "sa" designation meaning see also, other subjects which are more specific or narrower than "Scientific expeditions." 4. "x" designation referring to subject headings which are not used. 5. "xx" designation meaning see also, terms which are broader in scope than "Scientific expeditions." 6. Subdivision following a subject heading. 7. Cross reference from a subject not used to a subject heading that is used.

It may be seen that there are many possibilities for locating
similar materials under a variety of subjects. The designation (Indirect) after "Scientific expeditions" refers to the
addition of geographical subdivisions when appropriate. The
name of the relevant country is interposed between the subject entry and a local name such as a city, for example,
Scientific expeditions--Brazil--Mato Grosso.

Author Entries

Books are usually entered in the collection index under
individual authors, but they may appear listed under government departments (United States. Dept. of Transportation),
institutions (California Academy of Sciences, San Francisco),
associations (National Canners Association), or corporations
(Dow Chemical Company). An editor who has selected a group
of writings or a compiler who has done a lengthy bibliography
will have those books entered under his/her name. Occasionally
books are entered under their titles (Encyclopaedia Britannica)
or under the name of a meeting (Symposium on Supercomputers
and Chemistry (1980 : Las Vegas, Nev.)).

```
TJ
280.7  (1) Blair, Peter D.
.B55       Geothermal energy : investment
1982       decisions and commercial development /
       (2) Peter D. Blair, Thomas A.V. Cassel,
           Robert H. Edelstein. -- New York :
           Wiley, c1982.
           x, 184 p. : ill. ; 24 cm. --
           (Alternate energy)
           "A Wiley-Interscience publication."
           Bibliography: p. 172-180.
           Includes index.

           1. Geothermal engineering.
           2. Geothermal resources.  3. Energy
           policy.  I. Cassel, Thomas A. V.
           II. Edelstein, Robert H.  III. Title
           IV. Series

    CSLuSP ck/cs 820629 7740945  CPSMac      81-13139
```

1. Main author. 2. Co-authors (who will also have entries
in the catalog).

Title and Series Entries

```
                      Geothermal energy

TJ
280.7      Blair, Peter D.
.B55          Geothermal energy : investment
1982       decisions and commercial development /
           Peter D. Blair, Thomas A.V. Cassel,
           Robert H. Edelstein. -- New York :
           Wiley, c1982.
              x, 184 p. : ill. ; 24 cm. --
           (Alternate energy)
              "A Wiley-Interscience publication."
              Bibliography: p. 172-180.
              Includes index.

              1. Geothermal engineering.
           2. Geothermal resources.  3. Energy
           policy.  I. Cassel, Thomas A. V.
           II. Edelstein, Robert H.  III. Title
           IV. Series


CSLuSP                          CPSMtc      81-13139
```

Reprinted with permission of OCLC Online Computer Library Center, Inc.

```
                     Alternate energy.

TJ
280.7      Blair, Peter D.
.B55          Geothermal energy : investment
1982       decisions and commercial development /
           Peter D. Blair, Thomas A.V. Cassel,
           Robert H. Edelstein. -- New York :
           Wiley, c1982.
              x, 184 p. : ill. ; 24 cm. --
           (Alternate energy)
              "A Wiley-Interscience publication."
              Bibliography: p. 172-180.
              Includes index.

              1. Geothermal engineering.
           2. Geothermal resources.  3. Energy
           policy.  I. Cassel, Thomas A. V.
           II. Edelstein, Robert H.  III. Title
           IV. Series


CSLuSP                          CPSMtc      81-13139
```

Reprinted with permission of OCLC Online Computer Library Center, Inc.

Title Entries

Title entries are included for most books in library collections. The title heading "Geothermal energy" appears in the
upper example on the previous page over the author's name,
without the subtitle in this instance.

Series Entries

Series are also noted in the collection index when they are
significant. The series name "Alternate energy" appears as
a heading in the lower example on the preceding page. Additional information concerning the publication is given in
notes.

Filing

Filing rules vary from one library to another. There are a
few general observations that can be made regarding policies
in most libraries. The arrangement of entries in the index
may be alphabetical word-by-word or letter-by-letter. Personal names precede titles. Punctuation marks are disregarded.
Note this example of word-by-word filing compared to letter-
by-letter filing:

Word-by-Word	Letter-by-Letter
New, Stephen	New republic
New republic	New, Stephen
New York Times	New Yorker
New Yorker	New York Times

Initial articles such as an, the, a (both English and
foreign) are disregarded at the beginnings of titles.
Abbreviations and numbers may be filed as if they were
spelled out, or not, depending upon whether the filing
is done by a person, or by a computer. Initials, such
as C.I.A., and single letters are filed before a word
beginning with the same letter, like this:

    C and I
    C.I.A. and the cult of intelligence
    Cat in the hat

However, pronounceable acronyms such as ALGOL file as words:

    Algebra and you
    ALGOL
    Alleviating back pain

Library Classification Systems

Each book is classified, that is, given a classification (letter or number) code which designates its subject. Materials are arranged in libraries according to these codes, which are usually referred to as "call numbers." In this way the user can often find similar materials close together on library shelves. There are two major classification systems in use in the United States: the Dewey Decimal, which divides all knowledge into ten classes using numbers 0-9, and the Library of Congress scheme, which uses 21 letters of the alphabet for its major classifications.

Dewey	LC	SCIENCE
500	Q	Science (General)
510	QA	Mathematics
520	QB	Astronomy
530	QC	Physics
540	QD	Chemistry
550	QE	Geology
574.9	QH	Natural history (General)
580	QK	Botany
590	QL	Zoology
611	QM	Human anatomy
612	QP	Physiology
576	QR	Microbiology

		MEDICINE
616	R	Medicine (General)
614	RA	Public aspects of medicine
610-619	RC-RZ	Other topics in medicine

		AGRICULTURE
630	S	Agriculture (General)
633-635	SB	Plant culture
634.9	SD	Forestry
636-638	SF	Animal culture
639.2	SH	Aquaculture. Fisheries. Angling.
639.1	SK	Hunting

		TECHNOLOGY
600	T	Technology (General)
620	TA	Engineering (General). Civil engineering (General).
627	TC	Hydraulic engineering
628	TD	Sanitary engineering
625.7	TE	Highway engineering
625.1	TF	Railroad engineering
624.2	TG	Bridge engineering
690	TH	Building construction
621	TJ	Mechanical engineering

621.3	TK	Electrical engineering.
		Electronics.
621.48		Nuclear engineering.
622, 669	TN	Mining engineering. Metallurgy.
660	TP	Chemical technology
660-680	TS	Manufactures
640	TX	Home economics

Within each main classification in the Library of Congress system, books are further subdivided by a number which designates a narrower subject, and another number which usually represents the author, for example:

    QC = Physics
    481 = x-rays
    .B35 - author: Becker

Occasionally a year is added to indicate the edition. Books are arranged on the shelf alphabetically by the first letter of the call number, for example Q; again alphabetically within the Q section--Q, QA, QB, QC, etc.; then numerically by the integers directly below the letters, and lastly by the author numbers, which are decimals. Here is a set of call numbers in the correct order:

TN	TN	TP
283	283	245
.H61	.H7	.A7

In the Dewey Decimal system, the basic ten classes are divided into 1,000 more specific topics. By adding a decimal point and additional numbers, many more subdivisions are represented. Author numbers are added below the Dewey number, for example:

    540
    .Y85C

4
Previewing the Abstracts and Indexes

Abstracting and indexing services list citations to many
publications. Indexes include citations (listings of author,
title of article, journal, volume, pages, and year) only
while abstracting services have both citations and summaries
of the documents.

There are numerous abstracts and indexes to periodicals,
reports, symposia, proceedings, dissertations, review articles, and sometimes books in science, technology, and agriculture. The abstracts and indexes save much time in looking
up materials which would otherwise be almost impossible to
find. Usually the approach to finding these materials is
through some type of subject access (index). Also included
in most indexes is an author access. Once the access points
(indexes) are located, the next step is to find the citation.

How to Use the Abstracts and Index Sections

This chapter includes instructions on how to use the abstracts
and index chapters. There are three factors to be aware of:

I. Subject Areas and the One, Two, and Three Step Approaches

The table on the next few pages indicates areas and the pages
which have explanations of the corresponding abstracts and
indexes. In addition, the table indicates whether the index
has a "one step," "two step," or "three step" approach. In
the "one step" approach it is necessary to look in only one
place for the full citation. Readers' Guide to Periodical
Literature is an example of this type of index. In the "two
step" approach it is necessary to look two places in the
index or abstract in order to find the full citation. The
"two step" approach is much like a book with an index. The
first step is to look in the index at the back of the book.
The index refers to a page in the text of the book. This
page in the text represents the second step. Biological
Abstracts illustrates a "two step" subject approach in which

the first step is the subject index and the second step is
the abstract. Most abstracts are of the "two step" approach
for both author and subject.

In the "three step" process the first step may be to look at
a list of terms leading to a subject index in the second step.
The third step leads to the citation. Chemical Abstracts has
a "three step" approach to find a citation through the
subject.

The following lists the "step" categories.

    a. One step subject and author approach.

    b. Two step subject and author approach.

    c. Two step subject, one step author approach.

    d. One step subject, two step author approach.

    e. Three step subject approach, one step author
       approach.

    f. Three step subject approach, two step author
       approach.

SUBJECT AREAS AND THE ONE, TWO, AND THREE STEP APPROACHES

Subject Index or Abstract	One Step Subject	One Step Author	Two Step Subject	Two Step Author	Three Step Subject	Page
General						
American Statistics Index			X	X		85
CIS Annual			X			88
Comprehensive Dissertation Index	X					76
Conference Papers Index			X	X		71
Cumulative Subject Index to Monthly Catalog			X			84
Directory of Published Proceedings			X	X		72
Dissertation Abstracts International. Section B. Science and Engineering			X	X		77
General Science Index	X					34
Government Reports Announcements and Index			X	X		90
Index to Scientific & Technical Proceedings			X	X		74
Index to Scientific Reviews		X	X			66
Index to U.S. Government Periodicals			X	X		92

Subject Index or Abstract	One Step Subject, Author	Two Step Subject	Two Step Author	Three Step Subject	Page
Magazine Index	X				33
Monthly Catalog of U.S. Government Publications		X	X		81
Monthly Checklist of State Publications		X			93
Readers' Guide to Periodical Literature	X				34
Science Citation Index	X	X			35
Scientific and Technical Aerospace Reports		X	X		94
Agriculture					
Bibliography of Agriculture		X	X		40
Biological & Agricultural Index	X				34
Commonwealth Agricultural Bureaux Abstracting Services		X	X		41
Current Contents. Agriculture, Biology & Environmental Sciences		X	X		64

Subject — Index or Abstract	One Step Subject, Author	Two Step Subject	Two Step Author	Three Step Subject	Page
Biochemistry					
Biological Abstracts		X	X		43
Biological Abstracts/RRM		X	X		69
Biological & Agricultural Index	X				34
Chemical Abstracts			X	X	47
Current Contents. Life Sciences		X	X		64
Biology and Botany					
Biological Abstracts		X	X		43
Biological Abstracts/RRM		X	X		69
Biological & Agricultural Index	X				34
Current Contents. Agriculture, Biology & Environmental Sciences		X	X		64
Current Contents. Life Sciences		X	X		64
Chemistry					
Applied Science & Technology Index	X				34
Chemical Abstracts			X	X	47

Subject Index or Abstract	One Step Subject	Author	Two Step Subject	Author	Three Step Subject	Page
Current Contents. Life Sciences			X	X		64
Current Contents. Physical, Chemical & Earth Sciences			X	X		64
Computer Science						
Applied Science & Technology Index	X					34
Current Contents. Engineering, Technology & Applied Sciences			X	X		64
Science Abstracts. Series C. Computer and Control Abstracts			X	X		59
Engineering						
Applied Science & Technology Index	X					34
Current Technology Index		X	or	X		52
Current Contents. Engineering, Technology & Applied Sciences			X	X		64
Engineering Index	X			X		50
Science Abstracts. Series B. Electrical and Electronics Abstracts			X	X		59

Subject Index or Abstract	One Step Subject, Author	Two Step Subject, Author	Three Step Subject	Page
Mathematics				
Applied Science & Technology Index	X			34
Mathematical Reviews		X		53
Medicine				
Current Contents. Clinical Practice		X		64
Current Contents. Life Sciences		X		64
Excerpta Medica		X		58
Index Medicus	X		X	55
Physics and Geology				
Applied Science & Technology Index	X			34
Bibliography and Index of Geology		X		61
Current Contents. Physical, Chemical & Earth Sciences		X		64
Science Abstracts. Series A. Physics Abstracts		X		59

Subject / Index or Abstract	One Step Subject	One Step Author	Two Step Subject	Two Step Author	Three Step Subject	Page
Zoology						
Biological Abstracts			X	X		43
Biological Abstracts/RRM			X	X		69
Biological & Agricultural Index	X					34
Current Contents. Agriculture, Biology & Environmental Sciences			X	X		64
Current Contents. Life Sciences			X	X		64
Zoological Record		X			X	45

II. "Order of Search"

The following table illustrates the "order of search"
pattern. The "order of search" lists access points (indexes)
available in the indexes and abstracts. There may be several
access points available. For instance, Biological Abstracts
has five access points (see the following). The next step in
Biological Abstracts' "order of search" is to find the
abstract (step 2) for the full citation (this is a "two step"
approach). To state it another way, to find the topic
"chloroplasts," first look in the subject index (step 1.a.),
record the reference number, then turn to the abstract section (step 2) and find the abstract. The next step is to
write down the name of the journal, volume, pages, and date.

ORDER OF SEARCH FOR ABSTRACTS AND INDEXES

Example:

Biological Abstracts

Order of Search:

	①		② Reference no.
Step 1.a.	Subject Index	Record:	69197
or b.	Author Index	Record:	69197
or c.	Biosystematic Index	Record:	69197
or d.	Generic Index	Record:	69197
or e.	Concept Index	Record:	69197 ③
Step 2	Abstracts	Find:	69197
		Record:	citation

1. access points (indexes) 2. action to take
once the reference number is located
3. example of number to record or find

III. "Procedure for Using" the Index or Abstract

Another feature in the chapters on abstracts and indexes is
the "procedure for using" the index or abstract. The pages
for this procedure are designated in the table entitled
"Subject Areas and the One, Two, and Three Step Approaches."
Usually the "procedure for using" the index or abstract
describes the subject approach. The procedure outlines
examples taken from the abstracts or indexes themselves.

5
Locating the Major Sources of Information Through Abstracts and Indexes for the Major Disciplines

Introduction

Basic information is usually found in journal articles covering original research. Journal literature is considered to be the most important form of scientific writing. There are many abstracts and indexes, the majority of which index journal articles. They often index other types of literature such as reviews and proceedings as well. Usually they cover a subject area and are comprehensive in coverage.

All the indexes and abstracts included in this chapter index journal articles and almost all index other types of literature. A description, "order of search," and procedure for using each of the abstracts and indexes are included in this chapter. Computer retrieval services (databases) are tabulated in Appendix III. Additional listings of abstracts and indexes are found in Appendix I.

This chapter is divided by subjects beginning with those abstracts in general science. The remaining subject areas are arranged alphabetically.

Science, General

I. Magazine Index:

Magazine Index contains citations of over 370 popular journals, several of which come from popular science titles. It cumulates monthly on microfilm with as little as a two week lag period between the publication of a journal and the appearance of its citation in Magazine Index. The cumulations cover a five year period. The index's database is called MAGAZINE INDEX. Further information on this database may be found in Appendix III under "Science, Technology, and Agriculture."

Procedure for Using the Microfilm of Magazine Index

Consult the index for the subject and record the citation.

Sample entry from the microfilm of Magazine Index.

(1) BEETLES
            —RESEARCH
    (2) Beetles: dung ho! (using beetles to
        control manure) by Vietmeyer, Noel (3)
    (4)   il   Science'82 v3
                    July-Aug'82-p98(1) (5)

    1. subject heading 2. title of article
    3. author 4. illustrations, journal title,
       volume 5. month, year, page
Extract taken from the *Magazine Index*™ published by Information
Access Co.; Menlo Park, CA

II.   Wilson Company Indexes:

The H. W. Wilson Company indexes (Readers' Guide to Periodical
Literature, Biological & Agricultural Index, Applied Science &
Technology Index, and the General Science Index) are the least
complicated to use, and the journals indexed are a little less
specialized than those indexed by the more comprehensive
indexes and abstracts. The major disadvantage of the Wilson
indexes is the incomplete coverage of the literature. Each
index indexes about 200 magazines, so much material will be
missed if the search includes journals from only these
indexes. These indexes are arranged alphabetically by subject and the subjects are further subdivided for easy browsing.
Readers' Guide also has entries under the author of an article.

The H. W. Wilson Company is developing a database for its
indexes.
Readers' Guide to Periodical Literature is most suitable for
finding articles on popular topics for the lay person. Most
noteworthy of the science publications indexed are Science and
Scientific American.

General Science Index indexes science journals, the majority
of which are also indexed in some of the other Wilson Indexes.
Nature is included in this index, but not in Readers' Guide.

Applied Science & Technology Index includes chemistry, computer science, engineering, geology, mathematics, and physics.

Biological & Agricultural Index indexes the subjects of
biology, agriculture, and related sciences.

Procedure for Using the Biological & Agricultural Index

Consult the index for the subject and record the citation.

Sample entry from the Biological & Agricultural Index:

① HORSES, Age of
   Influence of season and age on reproductive activ-   ②
   ity in pony mares on the basis of a slaughter-
   house survey. J. A. Wesson and O. J. Ginther.   ③
④ bibl il J Animal Sci 52:119-29 Ja '81

1. subject   2. title of article   3. authors
4. bibliography, illustrations, journal title,
volume, pages, month, year

Biological & Agricultural Index, Copyright © 1981 by The H. W. Wilson
Company. Material reproduced by permission of the publisher.

III.   Science Citation Index:

Science Citation Index indexes more than 3600 source
journals and source publications and Science Citation Index,
Abridged Edition indexes more than 500 source journals in
science, technology, and agriculture. Not only are journal
articles included in Science Citation Index, but articles
from symposia, monographic series (reviews), and multi-
authored books are also included. Science Citation Index
is published every two months. It cumulates every year and
every five years. The records of Science Citation Index
are also on computer tapes to form the database SCISEARCH.
Further information on this database may be found in
Appendix III under "Science, Technology and Agriculture."

Science Citation Index - Subject Approach

Order of Search:

Subject Approach

		Author	
Step 1.	Permuterm Subject Index	Record:	SAKAI K
Step 2.	Source Index	Find:	SAKAI K
		Record:	citation

Procedure for Using the Subject Approach of Science Citation
Index

1.   Consult the Permuterm Subject Index and record the
     author.

Sample entry from the Permuterm Subject Index of Science Citation Index:

①DNA (CONT)
   LIVER ----- SAKAI K ②

1. term   2. coterm, authors

Reprinted with permission from *Science Citation Index®* January-February 1982 Bimonthly, copyright 1982. Copyright owned by the Institute for Scientific Information®, Philadelphia, PA, U.S.A.

2.   Use the Source Index, find the author, and record the citation.

Sample entry from the Source Index of Science Citation Index:

①SAKAI K
②MURATA N CHIBA K YAMANE Y--EFFECT OF COPPER
 ADMINISTRATION ON THE INCORPORATION OF (THYMIDINE- ③
 H-3 INTO THE LIVER DNA OF RATS STIMULATED BY
 DIMETHYL-NITROSAMINE AND DIETHYLNITROSAMINE
④ CARCINOGENE   2(12):1261-1266   81   27R
    CHIBA UNIV,FAC PHARMACEUT SCI, CHIBA 260, JAPAN ⑤

1. author 2. coauthor 3. title of article
4. journal title, volume, issue, pages, date,
number of references 5. first author's address

Reprinted with permission from *Science Citation Index®* January-February 1982 Bimonthly, copyright 1982. Copyright owned by the Institute for Scientific Information®, Philadelphia, PA, U.S.A.

A diagram of the subject approach is given below.

SUBJECT APPROACH

PERMUTERM SUBJECT INDEX
1.   FIND SUBJECT
2.   RECORD AUTHOR

SOURCE INDEX
3.   FIND AUTHOR
4.   RECORD CITATION

Pritchard, E.
"Teaching Science Citation Index for a Library Orientation." *Journal of Technical Writing & Communication* Vol. 9:4 1979 p. 299
© 1979, Baywood Publishing Co., Inc.

Science Citation Index - Citation Approach

Order of Search:

Citation Approach

		Cited author/		Citing author
Step 1.	Citation Index	Find: WATSON JD	Record:	CONNER BN
Step 2.	Source Index		Find:	CONNER BN
			Record:	citation

This unique approach allows one to take a key paper and find more current information relating to the key paper.

Procedure for Using the Citation Index of Science Citation Index

1. Consult the Citation Index for the name of an earlier author and his/her paper.

    Sample entry from the Citation Index of Science Citation Index:

① WATSON JD.......................
    53 NATURE 171   263
        FORSDYKE DR   J THEOR BIO   93   861   81
② 53 NATURE 171   737
    ③ CONNER BN   NATURE   295   294   82
        HAKOSHIM T   P MAS BIOL   78   7309   81
        UTSUMI KR   CELL STRUCT   N   6   395   81

1. cited author 2. year of cited author's paper, journal, volume, page 3. citing author, journal, volume, page, year

Full citation of cited author's paper:

Watson, J. D. and F. H. C. Crick. "Molecular Structure of Nucleic Acids. A Structure for Deoxyribose Nucleic Acids." Nature 171:737-38, 1953.

Full citation of citing author's paper:

Conner, B. N., T. Takano, S. Tanaka, K. Itakura, and R. E. Dickerson. "The Molecular Structure of d(^{I}CpCpGpG), a Fragment of Right-Handed Double Helical A-DNA." Nature 295:294-99, 1982.

J. D. Watson is the authority or cit*ed* author. He wrote an article in 1953 on DNA (deoxyribose nucleic acid) and later authors of articles, such as Conner, are listed below Watson's name as cit*ing* authors. The assumption is that the cit*ing* author who quoted Watson's paper will give more information on the subject of Watson's paper such as more recent information on DNA. This index allows one to trace information from an earlier idea to a more recent idea when only an older article is known.

2. Turn in the Source Index to the author and record the citation.

    Sample entry from the Source Index of Science Citation Index:

① CONNER BN
②   TAKANO T TAMAKA S ITAKURA K DICKERSO RE-THE
③   MOLECULAR-STRUCTURE OF D (ICPCPGPG), A FRAGMENT OF
        RIGHT-HANDED DOUBLE HELICAL A-DNA
④   NATURE   295(5847):294:299   82   27R
⑤   CALTECH, DIV CHEM & CHEM ENGH, PASADENA 82 9112⁵

    1. Cit*ing* author 2. coauthors 3. title of
    article 4. journal, volume, issue, pages, year,
    number of references 5. address of first author

The diagram below gives an outline to follow when using the citation approach.

CITATION APPROACH

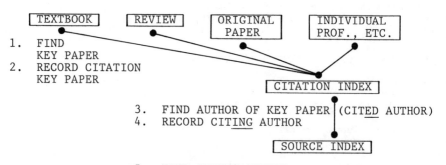

1. FIND
    KEY PAPER
2. RECORD CITATION
    KEY PAPER

    3. FIND AUTHOR OF KEY PAPER (CITED AUTHOR)
    4. RECORD CIT*ING* AUTHOR

    5. FIND CIT*ING* AUTHOR
    6. RECORD CI*T*ATION

Pritchard, E.
"Teaching Science Citation Index for a Library Orientation." *Journal of Technical Writing & Communication* Vol. 9:4 1979 p. 299
© 1979, Baywood Publishing Co., Inc.

Science Citation Index - Author Approach

Order of Search:

Author Approach

			Author
Step 1.	Source Index	Find:	SAKAI K
		Record:	citation

The author approach merely consists of looking for an author
in the Source Index (a one step process) which gives the full
citation.

Science Citation Index - Corporate Approach ⸝

Order of Search:

Corporate Approach

			Corporation or author
Step 1.	Corporate Index; Organization Section	Record:	ROCKWELL INT CORP CALIFORNIA ANAHEIM
Step 2.	Corporate Index; Geographic Section	Record:	WANG DC
Step 3.	Source Index	Find:	WANG DC
		Record:	citation

Science Citation Index - Patent Citation Approach

Order of Search:

Patent Citation Approach

		Patent no. & patentee/	Citing author
Step 1.	Patent Citation Index	Find: 4 151 127 PERNER J	Record: GALANTE DC
Step 2.	Source Index		Find: GALANTE DC Record: citation

Science Citation Index - Cycling Approach

The "cycling approach" is a sophisticated way of using the
Science Citation Index. It allows the searcher to find the
most recent papers through the use of the Citation Index and
older papers through the use of the citing author's "literature cited." Once the searcher finds an author and paper in
the "literature cited" he/she may return to the Citation
Index with that name and see who is citing that person; thus
the cycling is accomplished. This allows a thorough search
to be made using citations only.

Order of Search:

Cycling Approach

	Cited author/	Citing author/	Author found in journal bibliography
Step 1. Citation Index	Find: FRISCH KV	Record: JONES CE	
Step 2. Source Index		Find: JONES CE	
Step 3. Paper of citing author		Find: Jones, C.E.	Record: Straw, R.M.
Step 4. Citation Index	Find: STRAW RM	Record: LEVIN DA	

Agriculture

I. Bibliography of Agriculture:

Bibliography of Agriculture is published monthly, and its
index is cumulated yearly. This publication covers literature
collected by the National Agricultural Library. It includes
citations of journal articles, pamphlets, government documents (including extension and experiment station publications), special reports, and proceedings. Its contents are
in a database called AGRICOLA. Further information on this
database may be found in Appendix III under "Agriculture."

Order of Search:

		Citation no.	
Step 1.a.	Subject Index	Record:	081574
or b.	Personal Author Index	Record:	081574
or c.	Corporate Author Index	Record:	084241
or d.	Geographic Index	Record:	076332
Step 2.	Main Entry Section	Find:	081574
		Record:	citation

Procedure for Using the Subject Index of Bibliography of Agriculture

1. Consult the Subject Index and record the citation number.

    Sample entry from the Subject Index of the Bibliography of Agriculture:

① **DRAGONFLIES**
    Adult biology and behavior of the *dragonfly* **Tanypteryx** hageni (Odonata: Petaluridae). ②
③   081574

    1. subject heading 2. subject 3. citation number
    Reprinted with permission of The Oryx Press.

2. Turn to the Main Entry Section, find the citation number, and record the citation.

    Sample entry from the Main Entry Section of the Bibliography of Agriculture.

① 081574   420 K13
    Adult biology and behavior of the dragonfly ②
    Tanypteryx hageni (Odonata: Petaluridae).
③ Clement, S.L.; Meyer, R.P. *J Kans Entomol*
    Soc p. 711-719. ill. Oct 1980. v. 53 (4) ④

    1. citation number 2. title of article 3. authors, journal title 4. pages, illustrations, month, year, volume, issue
    Reprinted with permission of The Oryx Press.

II. Commonwealth Agricultural Bureaux:

The Commonwealth Agricultural Bureaux are organizations of the British Commonwealth nations producing international abstracting services dealing with agriculture and its related fields. The services provide citations from journals, abstracts, annotated bibliographies, review articles, proceedings, and books. CAB is the database for the 25 plus abstracting journals published by the Commonwealth Agricultural Bureaux. Their publications are issued every month and there are yearly cumulative indexes. Further information on this database may be found in Appendix III under "Agriculture."

<u>Horticultural Abstracts</u> (example of an abstracting service
from the Commonwealth Agricultural Bureaux)

Order of Search:

			Abstract no.
Step 1.a.	Subject Index	Record:	249
or b.	Author Index	Record:	249
Step 2.	Abstracts	Find:	249
		Record:	citation

<u>Procedure for Using the Subject Index of Horticultural</u>
<u>Abstracts</u>

1. Consult the Subject Index and record the abstract number.

    <u>Sample entry</u> from the Subject Index of the <u>Horticultural</u>
    <u>Abstracts</u>.

(1) **Grapevine**

    irrigation
       requirements, determination   8060
       responses   646, 2472, 6152, 8886
    juvenility, induction, tissue culture   3230
    layering, methods   8182
    leaf
       ascorbic acid   8195
       colour, fungicides   3227
       development, tissue culture   8197, 8198
       morphology, heat treatment   2470
       pigments, nutrition   6999
       potassium   8190
    light, spectral composition, responses
       3208
    manganese, nutrition   4115
    minor elements, nutrition   1756, 1757
    mulching   5084
    mycorrhiza   2479
    nematicides, application, equipment   6770
    nitrogen, nutrition   249, 961, 1755, 2476,   (2)
       3215, 3216, 3222, 6141, 6997, 6998,
       6999, 7679, 7685, 8188

    1. subject   2. abstract numbers

2. Turn to the Abstracts, find the abstract number, and record the citation.

Sample entry from the Abstracts of the Horticultural Abstracts:

(1) *Vines – soils and nutrition*

(2) 249   BELL, A. A.; OUGH, C. S.; KLIEWER, W. M.
(3) **Effects on must and wine composition, rates of fermentation, and wine quality of nitrogen fertilization of *Vitis vinifera* var. Thompson Seedless grapevines.** *American Journal of Enology* (4)
(5) *and Viticulture* (1979) **30** (2) 124-129 [En, 25 ref.] California University, Davis, California 95616. USA.

Thompson Seedless vines, in a vineyard not fertilized for the preceding 7 years, were treated for 3 years with various rates of N. Clarified grape juice was analyzed. The rates of fermentation, concentration of esters, and wine quality were dependent on the level of N fertilization. Fertilization with 112 kg N/ha was sufficient for the juice to have a rapid fermentation and the wine to be of good quality. Juice from vines not fertilized fermented more slowly, resulted in wines of poorer quality and was deficient in a number of chemical components.

1. subject   2. abstract number, authors   3. title of article   4. journal   5. year, volume, issue, pages, language, references, address of first author

Reprinted with permission of The Commonwealth Bureau of Horticulture and Plantation Crops.

Biological Sciences

I. Biological Abstracts

Biological Abstracts is issued every two weeks and its index is cumulated every six months. It indexes domestic and foreign journal articles and books. Chapters of books are indexed in Biological Abstracts/RRM. Biological Abstracts/RRM also covers biological literature such as reports, reviews, and meetings which do not appear in Biological Abstracts. Biological Abstracts and Biological Abstracts RRM have their files combined to form the database BIOSIS PREVIEWS. Further information on this database may be found in Appendix III under "Biology."

Order of Search:

		Reference no.	
Step 1.a.	Subject Index	Record:	69197
or b.	Author Index	Record:	69197
or c.	Biosystematic Index	Record:	69197
or d.	Generic Index	Record:	69197
or e.	Concept Index	Record:	69197
Step 2.	Abstracts	Find:	69197
		Record:	citation

Procedure for Using the Subject Index of Biological Abstracts

1. Consult the Subject Index and record the reference number.

    Sample entry from the Subject Index of Biological Abstracts.

①	②	③
TURATION OF PREDATOR	PREDATORS COMPETING FOR PREY AND	30762
YSTEM WITH EGG EATING	MATHEMATICS NEW BORN C	30775
GOUS ARTHROPODS AND	UNDER DIFFERENT PESTICIDE	31070
RONS ASSOCIATED WITH	PREDATORY BEHAVIOR ELICITED BY LATE	33520
/ THE LIFE HISTORY AND	EFFICIENCY OF RAVINIA-LHER	32580

1. subject context 2. keyword 3. reference number

Copyright Biological Abstracts © 1982
Biological Abstracts
v 73 (5) March 1, 1982 pp 3155 and E 195

2. Turn to the Abstracts, find the reference number, and record the citation.

    Sample entry from the Abstracts of Biological Abstracts.

① ③ ④ **30762.** BAZYKIN, A. D. (Inst. of Biophysics, Academy of Sciences of the USSR, USSR–142 292 Puscino.) STUD BIOPHYS 83(2): 123–130. 1981. [In Russ. with Russ. and Engl. summ.] **Predator–prey model with saturation of predator, predators competing for prey and competing preys.**—A 3–parameter modification of a classical Volterra predator–prey model is studied. A four–parameter structural portrait and phase portraits for corresponding parameter regions are constructed. Biological interpretation of results is given. ②

1. reference number, author, author's address
2. journal title, volume, issue, pages, date
3. language, title or article 4. abstract

Copyright Biological Abstracts © 1982
Biological Abstracts
v 73 (5) March 1, 1982 pp 3155 and E 195

II. Zoological Record:

Zoological Record is published in yearly sections. The sections deal with a specific group of animals such as Protozoa
or Mammalia. Zoological Record does not appear as promptly as
most indexes and abstracts, but it has an almost exhaustive
coverage of the literature in systematic zoology for the year
stated on the section cover. In other areas of zoology, the
coverage is more selective. The types of literature scanned
for articles include journals, books, reviews, and proceedings. Dissertation Abstracts International is also scanned.
The database for this index is called ZOOLOGICAL RECORD.
Further information on this database may be found in
Appendix III under "Biology."

A. Systematic Approach

	Page no./	Author
Step 1. Index to Genera	Record: 623	
Step 2. Systematic Index	Find: 623	Record: Horton, K. J.
Step 3. Author Index		Find: Horton, K. J.
		Record: citation

B. Subject Index Approach

	Page no./	Author
Step 1. Detailed Subject Index	Record: 372	
Step 2. Subject Index	Find: 372	Record: Edgar, A. T.
Step 3. Author Index		Find: Edgar, A. T.
		Record: citation

C. Author Approach

	Author
Step 1. Author index	Find: Edgar, A. T.
	Record: citation

There are several ways to use Zoological Record, but the most
often used is its systematic index, which lists the scientific
name (genus and species). This index is based on the hier-
archy of zoological classification of the animal kingdom; so
it is difficult to use for those who do not have a good
background in classification.

Procedure for Using the Systematic Index of Zoological
Record

1. Consult the proper section (section 18 for Aves in this
    example), and find the genus (Zonotrichia in this
    example) in the Index to Genera. Record the page number
    given.

    Sample entry from the Index to Genera of Zoological
    Record:

Zenaida	577	
Zenaidura	577	
Zimmerius	597	
Zonotricha	623	
① Zonotrichia	623	②
Zoothera	616	
Zosterops	620	

        1. genus   2. page
Reprinted with permission of the Zoological Society of London.

2. Turn to the page listed for the genus and find the genus.
    Note the higher categories of classification (Emberizinae
    in this example). These are needed when looking for a
    genus in older editions of Zoological Record. Record the
    author (or editor) and citation number.

    Sample entry from the Systematic Index of Zoological
    Record:

① **EMBERIZINAE**

② *Zonotrichia atricapilla*
③   Michigan
        Battle Creek
        First record for Michigan   ④ Horton, K.J. [Ed.] (3252)

        1. higher category of classification   2. genus,
        species   3. subject   4. editor, citation number
Reprinted with permission of the Zoological Society of London.

3. Turn to the Author Index, find the author (editor in this
    example) or the citation number, and record the citation.

    Sample entry from the Author Index of <u>Zoological Record</u>:

① Horton, K.J. [Ed.]
    A new bird for Michigan. ②
③ Michigan Audubon Newsl. **26**(1) 1978: 5, illustr.

    1. editor   2. title of article   3. journal,
    volume, issue, year, page, illustrations
Reprinted with permission of the Zoological Society of London.

    An editor is given in this example. Most entries
    in <u>Zoological Record</u> begin with an author.

<u>Procedure for Using the Editions of Zoological Record Which
Do Not Have an Index to Genera</u>

1. Consult the Systematic Index table of contents for a
    classification category (Emberizinae is an example)
    higher than a genus. Record the page number.

2. Turn to the page number given and search for the genus
    (<u>Zonotrichia</u> is an example) on that page or the following
    pages. Record the author (or editor) and citation number.

3. Turn to the Author Index, find the author (or editor) or
    the citation number, and record the citation.

Chemistry

I. Chemical Abstracts

<u>Chemical Abstracts</u> is the world's most comprehensive chemical
index in the English language. It is issued weekly. Every
six months a cumulative index appears. Collective indexes
cover five year periods or more. <u>Chemical Abstracts</u> indexes
journal articles, reviews, and symposia. Its database is
CA SEARCH or CAS. Further information on this database may
be found in Appendix III under "Chemistry."

Order of Search:

A. Subject Approach (Bound Volumes)

			Volume/Abstract no.
Step 1.	Index Guide	Record: term	
Step 2.	General Subject Index	Find: term	Record: 94:207783w
Step 3.	Abstracts		Find: 94:207783w
			Record: citation

B. Chemical Substance Approach (Bound Volumes)

			Volume/Abstract no.
Step 1.	Index Guide	Record: chemical	
Step 2.	Chemical Sub-stance Index	Find: chemical	Record: 94:207783w
Step 3.	Abstracts		Find: 94:207783w
			Record: citation

C. Formula Approach (Bound Volumes)

		Volume/Abstract no.
Step 1.	Formula Index	Record: 94:207783w
Step 2.	Abstracts	Find: 94:207783w
		Record: citation

D. Author Approach (Bound Volumes)

		Volume/Abstract no.
Step 1.	Author Index	Record: 94:207783w
Step 2.	Abstracts	Find: 94:207783w
		Record: citation

E. Patent Approach by Patent Number (Bound Volumes)

		Abstract no.
Step 1.	Numerical Patent Index	Record: 37824q
Step 2.	Abstracts	Find: 37824q
		Record: citation

F. Patent Approach by Corresponding Patent Number
    (Bound Volumes)

		Volume/Abstract no.
Step 1.	Patent Concordance Find: patent no. turn to corresponding patent no.	Record: 85:192884r
Step 2.	Abstracts	Find: 85:192884r
		Record: citation

G.   Approach in Unbound Volumes

		Abstract no.
Step 1.a.	Keyword Subject Index	Record: 176438v
or b.	Author Index	Record: 176438v
or c.	Patent Index	Record: 93:137267g
Step 2.	Abstracts	Find: *96:176438v
		Record: citation

*abstract number for subject and author

Procedure for Using the General Subject Index of Chemical
Abstracts

1.   Consult the Index Guide to obtain the proper subject
     heading.

     Sample entry from the Index Guide of Chemical Abstracts:

① **Nutrition, plant**
       See *Plant nutrition*
    NUTSPEC
       See *Computer program*
    Nuttallin
       See *2-Butenoic acid, 3-methyl-, 9,10-dihydro-⌐*
          8,8-dimethyl-2-oxo-2H,8H-benzo[1,2-b:3,⌐
          4-b']dipyran-9-yl ester [22397-17-7]

1. subject heading
Material reproduced from *Chemical Abstracts* and the *Chemical Abstracts
Index Guide* is copyrighted by the American Chemical Society. Used by
permission.

2.   Search for the subject heading in the General Subject
     Index.

     Sample entry from the General Subject Index of Chemical
     Abstracts:

① **Plant nutrition**
       copper
          diagnosis of deficiency in, in clover, 207783u ②
          of subterranean clover, phosphorus supply effect
          on, 207761k

1. subject   2. abstract number
Material reproduced from *Chemical Abstracts* and the *Chemical Abstracts
Index Guide* is copyrighted by the American Chemical Society. Used by
permission.

3. Turn to the Abstract Section, find the abstract number, and record the citation.

    Sample entry from the Abstract Section of Chemical Abstracts:

(1) 94: 207783u **Copper nutrition of subterranean clover (Tri⁼ folium subterraneum L. cv. Seaton Park). II. Effects of copper supply on distribution of copper and the diagnosis of copper deficiency by plant analysis.** Reuter, D. J.; (2)
(3) Robson, A. D.; Loneragan, J. F.; Tranthim–Fryer, D. J. (South Aust. Dep. Agric., Adelaide, 5001 Australia). *Aust. J. Agric. Res.* (4)
(5) 1981, 32(2), 267–82 (Eng). The effect of Cu supply on the distribution of Cu in Seaton Park subterranean clover was examd. from early vegetative growth to plant maturity in 1 greenhouse expt. and in a second expt. was assessed at early flowering. The Cu content of old leaf blades of Cu–adequate
(6) plants decreased progressively with senescence of the blades. Cu deficiency delayed senescence and export of Cu from the older blades so that both the relative and net changes were substantially smaller than for blades of Cu–adequate plants. However, Cu concns. in senesced leaf blades still reflected Cu supply. At full senescence these blades contained appreciable quantities and concns. of Cu which contrasted with the low levels found in senesced leaves of wheat and peanuts in previous studies. Cu concn. in whole plant tops was not satisfactory for diagnosing Cu deficiency, since the crit. concn. decreased with plant age and during late vegetative development Piper–Steenbjerg curvature developed in the relation between Cu concn. and yield. It is possible that the curvature resulted partly from unusually high concns. of Cu in the old petioles of severely deficient plants. Anal. of Cu in young leaf blades provided a sensitive means of diagnosing Cu deficiency in subterranean clover. The estd. crit. concn. for these blades (3 μg/g for max. growth) did not change with plant age, at least until early flowering. In early growth, the Cu concn. of young leaf blades may be used to forecast impending Cu deficiency.

1. volume, abstract number, title of article
2. first author 3. coauthors, address of first author 4. journal title 5. year, volume, issue, pages, language 6. abstract

Engineering

I. Engineering Index

Engineering Index covers the world's technological literature. Most citations are from journals, conferences, reports, and monographs. Engineering Index is issued every month and cumulated every year. It also has five year cumulations. COMPENDEX is the database for this index. Further information on this database may be found in Appendix III under "Engineering and Technology."

Order of Search:

A. Subject Approach

			Subject
Step 1.	Subject Index	Find:	DAMS, ARCH
		Record:	citation

B. Author Approach

			Abstract no.
Step 1.	Author Index	Record:	028147
Step 2.	Subject Index	Find:	028147
		Record:	citation

Procedure for Using the Engineering Index

Consult the index for the subject and record the citation.

Sample entry from the Engineering Index:

DAIRIES

① Effluent Treatment

② 028143 SOIL AS A MEDIUM FOR DAIRY LIQ-
UID WASTE DISPOSAL. The paper reports on a field
study to evaluate the effectiveness of a vegetative-soil
filter for disposal of dairy effluent. The liquid waste was
applied daily to tall fescue on a Hosmer silt loam.
Applying effluent to the soil for absorption without
③ runoff was found to eliminate the possibility of stream
pollution except during rainfall and snowmelt runoff.
The highest loading rate for this soil under the most
adverse climatic conditions was 0.43 cm/day. The
pollutants in the liquid waste were reduced significantly
by flowing over the vegetative-soil filter but not to
acceptable levels. After 1 year of liquid waste applica-
tion to the test site, perched ground-water samples
showed a 99% BOD_5 decrease and a 90% removal of
PO_4-P. 13 refs.

④ Shen-Yi Yang (South Ill Univ, Carbondale, USA);   ⑤
⑥ Jones, Joe H.; Olsen, Farrel J.; Paterson, John J. J
Environ Qual v 9 n 3 Jul-Sep 1980 p 370-372.

1. subject   2. abstract number, title of article
3. abstract 4. first author, first author's address
5. coauthors 6. journal title, volume, issue, month,
year, pages

II.   Current Technology Index (formerly British Technology Index)

Current Technology Index is issued monthly and cumulated yearly. It indexes journal articles in engineering and chemical technology. For a complete list of topics, see "Outline of Subject Fields Covered" in the yearly volume. The files of Current Technology Index are not available as an online database.

Order of Search:

A.   Subject Approach

		Subject
Step 1. Subject Guide	Find:	PETROLEUM
	Record:	citation

B.   Author Approach

		Subject
Step 1. Author Index	Record:	PETROLEUM
Step 2. Subject Guide	Find:	PETROLEUM
	Record:	citation

Procedure for Using the Current Technology Index

Consult the Subject Guide for the subject and record the citation.

Sample entry from Subject Guide of Current Technology Index:

(1) **PETROLEUM : Drilling, Off shore : Diving : Equipment**
    How offshore oil has shaped diving support systems, pt.1. B. Molland. (2)
    (3) *Offshore Serv. Technol.*, 13 (Oct 80) p.38 +. *il.*

1. subject   2. title of article, author
3. journal title, volume, month, year,
pages, illustrations

Mathematics

I. Mathematical Reviews

Mathematical Reviews is published monthly. The index cumulates yearly and sometimes twice yearly. Mathematical Reviews
includes citations from journals, proceedings, and advanced
books in English, French, and German. The files of Mathematical Reviews are now available in the database called MATHFILE.
Further information on this database may be found in
Appendix III under "Mathematics."

Order of Search:

A. Subject Approach (Bound Volumes)

		Location no./ Record:	Abstract no.
Step 1.	Subject Classi- fication	14-XX: 14Hxx: 14H45	
Step 2.	Subject Index	Find : 14-XX: 14Hxx: 14H45	Record: 80c:14022
Step 3.	Abstracts		Find: 80c:14022 Record: citation

B. Author Approach (Bound Volumes)

		Abstract no.
Step 1.a.	Author Index	Record: 80c:14022
or b.	Key Index	Record: 80c:14002
Step 2	Abstracts	Find: *80c:14022 Record: citation

C. Subject and Author Approach (Unbound Volumes)

		Location no. or abstract no.
Step 1.a.	Table of Contents	Record: 14
or b.	Author Index	Record: 14006
Step 2.	Abstracts	Find: 82e:14006 Record: citation

*example of abstract number from Author Index.

Procedure for Using the Subject Index of Mathematical Reviews

1. Consult the Subject Classification Scheme and record the
    location number.

    Sample entry from AMS (MOS) Subject Classification Scheme
    of Mathematical Reviews:

14–XX   ALGEBRAIC GEOMETRY
14Hxx   Curves
    14H05   Algebraic functions [See also 14K20, 32G20.]
    14H10   Families, moduli (algebraic)
    14H15   Families, moduli (analytic) [See also 30F10, 32G15,
             32G20.]
    14H20   Singularities, local rings [See also 13Hxx.]
    14H25   Arithmetic ground fields [See also 10Bxx, 14Gxx.]
    14H30   Coverings, fundamental group
    14H35   Correspondences [See also 14Exx.]
    14H40   Jacobians [See also 32G20.]
(1) 14H45   Special curves
    14H99   None of the above, but in this section

1. location number to record

2. Find the location number in the Subject Index and record
    the abstract number.

    Sample entry from the Subject Index of Mathematical
    Reviews:

(1) 14H45   Special curves

   Arbarello, Enrico (*with* Sernesi, Edoardo) Petri's approach to the study of the ideal
      associated to a special divisor. **80c:14020**
(2) **Tannenbaum, Allen**   On the geometric genera of projective curves. **80c:14022**

1. location number   2. author, title of article,
abstract number

3. Turn to the abstracts, find the abstract number, and
    record the citation.

    Sample entry from the abstracts of <u>Mathematical Reviews</u>:

(1) **Tannenbaum, Allen**   (2) 80c:14022
    On the geometric genera of projective curves. (3)
(4)   *Math. Ann.* **240** (1979), *no.* 3, 213–221.

      A classical problem in algebraic geometry is to determine the
(5) possible genera of irreducible curves of degree *d* in $\mathbf{P}^n$, where the
    genus may be taken to be either the arithmetic genus or the
    geometric genus. In 1889, Castelnuovo gave an upper bound
    $\pi(d; n)$ for either; the present author shows that all geometric
    genera between 0 and $\pi(d; n)$ do in fact occur by exhibiting curves
    in $\mathbf{P}^n$ of degree *d* and arithmetic genus $\pi(d; n)$ possessing any
    number of nodes from 0 to $\pi(d; n)$. (The techniques of the paper
    apply more generally to the question of when there exist integral
    curves in a given linear equivalence class on a rational surface
    possessing a given number of nodes.) It should be noted that the
    question regarding arithmetic genera of curves in $\mathbf{P}^n$ is of a differ-
    ent character and still remains open.
                                    (6) *Joseph Harris* (Providence, R.I.)

    1. author 2. title of article 3. journal title,
    volume, year, issue, pages 4. abstract
    5. abstractor

                            Medicine

I.   Index Medicus

Index Medicus is produced by the National Library of Medicine
and is published monthly. It is composed of citations from
the literature of biomedical research and clinical medicine.
Cumulative volumes are produced once a year. Citations
include journal articles, reviews, editorials, biographies,
and obituaries. The database for Index Medicus is MEDLINE.
Further information on this database may be found in
Appendix III under "Medicine."

Order of Search:

A. Subject Approach

                                            Subject/Subject no.

Step 1.	Medical Subject Headings, Alphabetical List	Record: AGING G7.168+
Step 2.	Medical Subject Headings, Tree Structures	Find: AGING G7.168+
Step 3.	Subject Index	Find: AGING Record: citation

B. Author Approach

                                                          Author

Step 1.	Author Index	Find: Stupfel M Record: citation

Procedure for Using the Subject Index of Index Medicus

1. Consult the alphabetical list entitled Medical Subject Headings for the subject.

    Sample entry from the alphabetical list of Medical Subject Headings of Index Medicus:

(1) **AGING** (2)
     G7.168+
     X   SENESCENCE

AGITATION, PSYCHOMOTOR see PSYCHOMOTOR AGITATION

AGMATINE see under GUANIDINES

AGNOGENIC MYELOID METAPLASIA see MYELOID METAPLASIA

AGNOSIA
     C10.597.44+   C23.888.592.43+
     F3.126.185.794.118

AGONISTIC BEHAVIOR see under AGGRESSION

AGORAPHOBIA see under PHOBIC DISORDERS

    1. subject   2. tree structure number
National Library of Medicine

2. To see how the above chosen subject relates to broader
    and narrower terms in a hierarchical arrangement, consult
    the tree structures by noting the number given in the
    first list and tracing it to the second list.

    Sample entry from the Tree Structures of Index Medicus:

PHYSIOLOGY, GENERAL (NON MESH)	**G7**
ADAPTATION, PHYSIOLOGICAL	**G7.62**
ACCLIMATIZATION	**G7.62.133**
ESTIVATION ·	**G7.62.415**
HIBERNATION	**G7.62.592**
① **AGING**	② **G7.168**
AGE FACTORS	**G7.168.142**
GESTATIONAL AGE	**G7.168.383**
LONGEVITY	**G7.168.519**
MATERNAL AGE	**G7.168.590**
PATERNAL AGE	**G7.168.700**
PUBERTY	**G7.168.818**

1. subject 2. tree structure number
National Library of Medicine

3. Using the proper subject heading, turn to the Subject
    Index, find the citation, and record it.

    Sample entry from the Subject Index of Index Medicus:

① **LONGEVITY**
      see related
        LIFE EXPECTANCY
② Interindividual factors in respiratory behavior and longevity
      in OF1 mice. Stupfel M, et al. **Physiol Behav** 1981 Mar; ③
④ 26(3):517-24

1. subject 2. title of article 3. author,
journal title, year, month 4. volume, issue,
pages
National Library of Medicine

II.   Excerpta Medica

Excerpta Medica has 51 separate abstract journals with over 3500 biomedical publications indexed.   The publications are issued monthly with yearly cumulative indexes.   They cover publications throughout the world.   These abstract journals cover journal articles and occasionally review articles. EXCERPTA MEDICA is the database for this series of abstracts. Further information on this database may be found in Appendix III under "Medicine."

Excerpta Medica. Endocrinology

Order of Search:

		Abstract no.
Step 1.a.	Subject Index	Record: 1399
or b.	Author Index	Record: 1399
Step 2	Abstracts	Find: 1399
		Record: citation

Procedure for Using the Subject Index of Excerpta Medica. Endocrinology

1.   Consult the Subject Index and record the abstract number.

   Sample entry from the Subject Index of Excerpta Medica. Endocrinology

(1) **glycerol,** body weight, hunger, obesity, 5 patients, 1399 (2)
glycogen, acetylsalicylic acid, diabetes mellitus, free fatty acid, glucose
   - cyclic amp, insulin, fibroblast culture, bhk 21 cells, 1316
glycogen storage disease, fructose, glucagon, glucose, 2 cases, 1337
goiter, echography, hyperparathyroidism, parathyroid localization, 27
   - hyperthyroidism, iodine 131, thyroid adenoma, thyroid carcinoma
   - thyroid cancer, thyroid therapy, thyrotropin, review, 1260

   1. subject   2. abstract number
Reprinted with permission of *Excerpta Medica.*

2. Turn to the Abstract Section, find the abstract number, and record the citation.

Sample entry from the Abstract Section of Excerpta Medica. Endocrinology:

(1) **1399. Effect of glycerol on weight loss and hunger in obese patients** - Leibel R.L., Drewnowski A. and (2) (3) Hirsch J. - Lab. Hum. Behav. Metab., Rockefeller Univ., New York, N.Y. USA - *METAB. CLIN. EXP.* 1980 (4) (5) 29/12 (1234-1236)
(6) The effectiveness of oral glycerol as a dietary component or as a supplement to a 1000-kcal/day diet was examined in two studies involving obese patients. Glycerol did not differ from an equicaloric dose of glucose in its effect on hunger ratings, diet compliance or overall weight loss. We conclude that oral glycerol is not a useful adjunct to weight reduction programs.

1. abstract number   2. title of article   3. authors, first author's address   4. journal title, year, volume, issue, pages

Reprinted with permission of *Excerpta Medica*.

Physics and Geology

I.   Science Abstracts

Science Abstracts. Series A. Physics Abstracts is issued twice a month. The other two abstracts in this series, Computer & Control Abstracts and Electrical & Electronic Abstracts, are issued once a month. The subject indexes cumulate annually. Citations are taken from a wide range of publications including journals, reports, dissertations, books and conferences which are worldwide in their origin. Science Abstracts are available as a database called INSPEC. Further information on this database may be found in Appendix III under "Science and Technology."

<u>Science Abstracts.   Series A.   Physics Abstracts</u>

Order of Search:

A.   Unbound Issue Approach

		Abstract no./	Classi- fication no. /	Page
Step 1.a.	Subject Guide	Record:	0320	
or b.	Classification and Contents	Record:		0400
or c.	Author Index	Record: 41826		
or d.	Bibliographic Index	Record: 42639		
or e.	Book Index	Record: 38377		
or f.	Conference Index	Record: 38680		
or g.	Corporate Author Index	Record: 39160		
Step 2.	Abstracts	Find: 39160 or 0320 or 0400 Record: citation		

B.   Bound Issue Approach

			Year/	Abstract no.
Step 1.a.	Subject Index	Record: 1		93411
or b.	Author Index	Record: 1		93411
Step 2.	Abstracts	Find: (1981)		93411
		Record: citation		

<u>Procedure for Using the Subject Index of Science Abstracts.</u>
<u>Series A.   Physics Abstracts</u>

1.   Consult the Subject Index and record the abstract number.

<u>Sample entry</u> from the Subject Index of <u>Physics Abstracts</u>:

(1) **wind power**
    reliability of wind power systems in the UK 1−93411 (2)
    Rumanian nonconventional resources potential and technological prognosis
    (Rumanian) 1−66206

1. subject   2. year, abstract number

2.   Turn to the abstracts, find the abstract number, and
     record the citation.

     Sample entry from the abstracts of Physics Abstracts:

① ② ④ 93411   **The reliability of wind power systems in the UK.**   K.Newton
(Cavendish Lab., Univ. of Cambridge, Cambridge, England).
Wind Eng. (GB), vol.5, no.1, p.46-55 (1981). [received: May 1981] ③
A methodology has been developed to evaluate the performance of geographi-
cally distributed wind power systems. Results are presented for 3 widely
separated sites based on measured meteorological data obtained over a 17-yr
period. The effects of including energy storage were investigated and 150-hr
storage found to be a good compromise between store capacity and system
performance. (21 refs.)

     1. abstract number, title, author   2. author's
     address   3. journal title, volume, issue, pages,
     year, date received   4. abstract

II.   Bibliography and Index of Geology (American Geological
      Institute

Bibliography and Index of Geology is a monthly publication
which cumulates annually. It deals with the world's earth
science literature. It indexes books, journals, reviews,
reports, and maps. These are also included for North America.
The database, GEOREF, includes this index. Further information on this database may be found in Appendix III under
"Geology."

Order of Search:

A.   Approach in Unbound Issues

		Citation no./	Page
Step 1.a.	Subject Index	Record: 16076	
or b.	Table of Contents	Record:	834
or c.	Author Index	Record: 16076	
Step 2.	Fields of Interest	Find: 16076 or	834
		Record: citation	

B.   Subject Approach in Bound Volumes

		Author
Step 1.	Cumulative Index	Record: Sancer, E.V.
Step 2.	Cumulative Bibliography	Find: Sancer, E.V.
		Record: citation

C. Author Approach in Bound Volumes

		Author
Step 1. Cumulative Bibliography	Find:	Sancer, E.V.
	Record:	citation

Procedure for Using the Subject Index of Bibliography and
Index of Geology

1.   Consult the Subject Index and record the citation number.

Sample entry from the Subject Index of Bibliography and
Index of Geology:

(1) **Washington—volcanology**
   Mount Saint Helens:
   — Eruption of Mt. St. Helens; Effects on climate 16076 (2)

1. subject   2. citation number

Bibliography and Index of Geology
Copyright © by the American Geological Institute.

2.   Turn to the Fields of Interest section, find the citation number and record the citation.

Sample entry from the Fields of Interest section of Bibliography and Index of Geology:

(1)
(2)   16076 **Sear, C. B.; and Kelly, P. M.** Eruption of Mt. St.
(3)   Helens; Effects on climate: Nature, Vol. 285, p. 533-535, illus., June 19, 1980.

1. citation number, authors, title of article
2. journal title, volume, pages   3. illustrations,
month, day, year

Bibliography and Index of Geology
Copyright © by the American Geological Institute.

6
Locating the Abstracts and Indexes for Current Material, Reviews, Conference Proceedings, and Dissertations

Introduction

In this chapter the authors discuss special types of
materials which provide contributions to research. The
chapter is divided into three sections covering three types
of materials. Particularly important is finding the most
current material which is not possible using the indexes and
abstracts mentioned in Chapter 5 because of a publication
lag. Reviews and conference proceedings are sometimes in
the indexes and abstracts mentioned in Chapter 5, but there
are some exceptions. Dissertations are usually not included
in those indexes already discussed.

Obtaining the Most Current Information

The researcher usually wants the latest material on a topic.
Most indexes are months in appearing, especially where
writing new abstracts and editorial review are involved.

One may benefit from reading and scanning the journals in
a major field. Ulrich's Periodicals Directory lists the
major periodicals in the world by subject; the Science
Citation Index also contains lists of journals by subject.
Some representative journals are included in the lists in
Appendix II.

When the journal is not available for scanning, the user may
wish to look through Current Contents. The Current Contents
publications are especially designed to assist individuals
in keeping up with the literature.

I. Current Contents

Current Contents covers several fields which include science, technology and agriculture. The copies consist of reproduced tables of contents. Most of the index is devoted to journals, but the contents of separately published symposia, reviews and books are also included. Current Contents is particularly useful because it covers the most recent issues of journals--at about the same time that the journal comes out; thus it includes literature too recent to be found in other indexes. Current Contents. CompuMath and Current Contents. GeoSciTech appear monthly and are lacking subject and author indexes. The remaining Current Contents publications are issued weekly. They contain a "Weekly Subject Index" and an "Author Index & Address Directory." Current Contents is partially covered in the SCISEARCH database. Further information on this database may be found in Appendix III under "Science, Technology and Agriculture." Current Contents. CompuMath is included in the database ISI/ CompuMath.TM Further information on this database may be found in Appendix III under "Mathematics." Current Contents. GeoSciTech is included in the database ISI/GeoSciTech.TM Further information on this database may be found in Appendix III under "Geology."

Listed below are the Current Contents titles:

   Current Contents. Agriculture, Biology &
      Environmental Sciences

   Current Contents. Clinical Practice

   Current Contents. CompuMath

   Current Contents. Engineering, Technology &
      Applied Sciences

   Current Contents. GeoSciTech

   Current Contents. Life Sciences

   Current Contents. Physical, Chemical &
      Earth Sciences

   Current Contents. Social & Behavioral Sciences

Order of Search:

		CC page/Journal page	
Step 1.a.	Journal indexed in issue ("In this issue")	Record: 46	
or b.	Weekly Subject Index	Record: 46	145
or c.	Author Index & Address Directory	Record: 46	
Step 2.	Reproduced journal contents page	Find: 46	
		Record: citation	

Procedure for Using the Weekly Subject Index of Current
Contents

1.   Consult the Weekly Subject Index and record the Current
     Contents page and journal page number.

     Sample entry from the Subject Index of Current Contents.
     Life Sciences:

1. subject   2. Current Contents page
3. journal page

2.   Turn to the Current Contents page and find the journal
     page number and record the citation.

     Sample entry from the contents section of Current Contents.
     Life Sciences:

① (NL455) **MEDICAL HISTORY** ②
Abstracts in English
③ VOL. 26 NO. 2   APRIL 1982

Articles

Physicians and the chemical analysis of mineral waters in
  eighteenth-century England, by NOEL G. COLEY   123

④ Suxamethonium – the development of a modern drug
  from 1906 to the present day, by HUW R. DORKINS   145 ⑤

John Addenbrooke, M.D. (1680–1719), by ARTHUR ROOK
  and LAWRENCE MARTIN   169

Porphyria revisited, by LINDSAY C. HURST   179

1. ISI accession number   2. title of journal
3. volume, issue, date   4. title of article,
author   5. journal page

Using Reviews and Conference Proceedings
for Background Information

Review articles, when available, are useful in providing an
overview of a specific topic. It can be advantageous to
find a review article at the beginning of a search. Once
the user knows how to use Index to Scientific Reviews, this
is a good reference to search. Other abstracts and indexes
devoted primarily to listing journal articles may also list
review articles. Biological Abstracts/RRM (Bioresearch
Index) has review citations. Chemical Abstracts identifies
review citations by placing an "R" in front of the abstract
number. Science Citation Index includes an "R" in the Source
Index to identify review article citations. Both Index
Medicus and Science Abstracts have special index sections
for review article citations, "Bibliography of Medical
Reviews" and "Bibliography Index" respectively.

Sometimes it may be necessary to search individual review
publications. Appendix IV lists, by subject, some of those
publications which are devoted entirely to reviews. Review
sources may also be found, listed by subject, in Irregular
Serials & Annuals: An International Directory.

Symposia or conference proceedings are sometimes difficult
to locate. Biological Abstracts/RRM (Bioresearch Index)
indexes separately each article in a collection of proceedings. The Directory of Published Proceedings does not, but
covers a broader area in science and technology. Conference
Papers Index covers the fields of life science, physical
science, and engineering, and indexes the chapters in the
proceedings by author and subject. The publication Index to
Scientific and Technical Proceedings has several access
points.

II.   Index to Scientific Reviews

The Index to Scientific Reviews indexes reviews from review
serials and review journals. Also considered for indexing
are articles from Science Citation Index which have 40 or
more references, an "R" (indicating a review or bibliography),
or titles with keywords such as "advances, review, or
progress." These candidates from Science Citation Index are
screened for the final list. All articles with 70 or more
references from Science Citation Index are automatically
included in the Index to Scientific Reviews. Over 2900
journals and serials of the world are indexed in Index to
Scientific Reviews. This index appears semiannually and
cumulates annually.

Order of Search:

A. Citation Approach

			Cited author/		Citing author
Step 1.	Citation Index	Find:	WATSON JD	Record:	BARBIN A
Step 2.	Source Index			Find:	BARBIN A
				Record:	citation

B. Subject Approach

			Author
Step 1.	Permuterm Subject Index	Record:	HOOGLAND JL
Step 2.	Source Index	Find:	HOOGLAND JL
		Record:	citation

C. Author Approach

			Author
Step 1.	Source Index	Find:	HOOGLAND JL
		Record:	citation

D. Corporate Approach

			Author
Step 1.	Corporate Index	Record:	VOGEL WM
Step 2.	Source Index	Find:	VOGEL WM
		Record:	citation

E. Patent Citation Approach

			Patent no. & patentee/		Citing author
Step 1.	Patent Cita- tion Approach	Find:	2 003 294, ALLUM KG	Record:	BAILEY DC
Step 2.	Source Index			Find:	BAILEY DC
				Record:	citation

F. Cycling Approach

			Cited author/		Citing author/	Author found in journal bibliography
Step 1.	Citation Index	Find:	FRISCH KV		Record:	BURGHARD GM
Step 2.	Source Index				Find:	BURGHARD GM
Step 3.	Paper of citing author				Find: Record:	Burghard, G.M. Lorenz, K.
Step 4.	Citation Index	Find:	LORENZ K		Record:	WEISFELD GE

Procedure for Using the Permuterm Subject Index of Index to
Scientific Reviews

1. Consult the Permuterm Subject Index and record the
    author's name.

    Sample entry from the Permuterm Subject Index of
    Index to Scientific Reviews:

    (1) EVOLUTION

            EVOLUTION (CONT)
              DIFFERENT -- KAFATOS M
              DIMORPHISM - ANDERSSO.M
              DISCOMYCET - SMITHSKAY.MF
              DISRUPTIVE - UDOVIC D
              DISSIPATIVE- GOBBI A
              DIVERGENCE - MIYATA T
    (2)   DOGS - - - - HOOGLAND JL
              DROSOPHILA - DICKINSO.WJ

        1. term   2. co-term, author

2. Turn to the Source Index and find the author and record
    citation.

    Sample entry from the Source Index of Index to
    Scientific Reviews:

HOOGLAND JL (1)
(2) THE EVOLUTION OF COLONIALITY IN WHITE-TAILED AND
    BLACK-TAILED PRAIRIE DOGS (SCIURIDAE, CYNOMYS-LEUCURUS
    AND CYNOMYS-LUDOVICIANUS)
(3) ECOLOGY   62(1):252-272   81   120R
(4)   UNIV MINNESOTA,JAMES FORD BELL MUSEUM NAT HIST.
       MINNEAPOLIS, MN 55455, USA

        1. author   2. title of article   3. journal, volume,
        issue, pages, year, number of references
        4. address of author

III. Biological Abstracts/RRM:

Biological Abstracts RRM (formerly Bioresearch Index) appears semimonthly and cumulates semiannually. It is a companion to Biological Abstracts and indexes foreign and domestic bio-logical publications. Biological Abstracts/RRM includes biological literature such as reports, reviews, and meetings. Books are broken down into chapters. Biological Abstracts and Biological Abstracts/RRM combine files to form the data-base BIOSIS PREVIEWS. Further information on this database may be found in Appendix III under "Biology."

Order of Search:

		Reference no.	
Step 1.a.	Subject Index	Record:	19218
or b.	Author Index	Record:	19218
or c.	Biosystematic Index	Record:	19218
or d.	Generic Index	Record:	19218
or e.	Concept Index	Record:	19218
Step 2.	Citations	Find:	19218
		Record:	citation

Procedure for Using the Subject Index of Biological Abstracts/RRM

1. Consult the Subject Index and record the citation number.

Sample entry from the Subject Index of Biological Abstracts/RRM:

①	②		③
ING BLOOD LIVER SPLEEN	ADRENAL	/THE EFFECT OF DIETARY VITA	17782
LDO STERONISM HUMAN		ADENOMA/ SCREENING FOR SU	20934
ANTAGONISTS DECREASE		AND VASCULAR RESPONSIVENE	19232
ICO STERONE/ PITUITARY		AXIS DURING TRANS SPHENOID	20992
YPOTHALAMO PITUITARY		AXIS IN BRAIN TUMORS ABSTRA	20835
IC FUNCTIONS OF BOVINE		CORTEX CELLS MAINTAINED IN	19242
RETICULAR ZONE OF THE		CORTEX IN THE EARLY PERIOD	20423
L HYPERTENSION REVIEW		CORTEX MINERALO. CORTICOID	18532
ONE/ ENHANCEMENT OF		FUNCTION BY OVINE TERM PLA	19235
YPOTHALAMO PITUITARY		FUNCTION DURING DEVELOPME	19227
N OF THE PRIMATE FETAL		GLAND AND GONAD HUMAN RH	19218
TION LIVER KIDNEY LUNG		GLAND PANCREAS TONSILS NE	20479

1. subject context   2. keyword   3. reference number

2. Turn to the citation section, find the reference number, and record the citation.

Sample entry from the citation section of Biological Abstracts/RRM:

① 19218. JAFFE, ROBERT B., MARIA SERON-FERRE, KENT CRIC⁼ KARD, DONALD KORITNIK, BRYAN F. MITCHELL and ILPO T.
② HUHTANIEMI. (Reprod. Endocrinol. Cent., Dep. Obstet. Gynecol. Reproductive Sci., Univ. Calif., San Francisco, Calif.) Greep, R. O. (Ed.). Recent Progress ③
④ in Hormone Research, Vol. 37. Proceedings of the 1980 Laurentian Hormone Conference, Mont Tremblant, Quebec, Canada, Aug. 24–29, 1980. xii+713p. ⑤
⑥ Academic Press, Inc., Publishers: New York, N.Y., USA; London, England. Illus. ISBN 0-12-571137-9. p41–104. 1981. **Regulation and function of the** ⑦ **primate fetal adrenal gland and gonad.**/HUMAN, RHESUS MONKEY,
⑧ CHORIONIC GONADOTROPIN, ACTH, MSH, DEHYDROEPIANDRO⁼ STERONE, CORTISOL, CORTISONE, STEROID PRODUCTION, HIS⁼ TOLOGY
⑨ CON: Histological & Histochemical Methods/Gonad & Placenta Studies/ Sterol,Steroid Metabolism/Descriptive Embryology/Pituitary Studies
⑩ TAX: Cercopithecidae/Hominidae

19219. NEW, MARIA I.*, BO DUPONT, SONGJA PANG*, MARILYN POLLACK and LENORE S. LEVINE*. (Div. Pediatr. Endocrinol., Dep. Pediatr., New York Hosp.–Cornell Med. Cent., New York, New York.) Greep, R. O. (Ed.). Recent Progress in Hormone Research, Vol. 37. Proceedings of the 1980 Laurentian Hormone Conference, Mont Tremblant, Quebec, Canada, Aug. 24–29, 1980. xii+713p. Academic Press, Inc., Publishers: New York, N.Y., USA; London, England. Illus. ISBN 0-12-571137-9. p105–182. 1981. **An update of congenital adrenal hyperplasia.**/HUMAN,

1. reference number, authors 2. author, first author's address 3. address, editor, title of series 4. volume of series, conference title 5. address of conference, date of conference, number of pages of conference publication 6. publishers, address where publication can be ordered 7. pages of the conference paper, date of publication, title of paper 8. subject terms 9. concepts 10. taxonomic names

IV.   Conference Papers Index

Conference Papers Index.   Life Sciences, Physical Sciences,
Engineering indexes papers presented at meetings, including
unpublished papers.   Approximately 100,000 papers are cited
each year.   The Index appears monthly, and cumulates yearly.
The subjects covered include engineering, biology, medicine,
chemistry, animal science, plant science, geoscience,
mathematics, computer science, pharmacology, physics,
astronomy, and multidisciplinary science fields.   Not all
fields are included in a single monthly issue, however.
The database for this index is CONFERENCE PAPERS INDEX.
Further information on this database may be found in
Appendix III under "Science and Technology."

Order of Search:

Approach for Conference Papers Index.   Life Sciences,
Physical Sciences, Engineering

		Year/Abstract no.
Step 1.a.	Subject Index	Record: 82-008752
b.	Author Index	Record: 82-008752
Step 2	Citation Section	Find: 82-008752
		Record: citation

Procedure for Using Subject Index of Conference Papers Index
Life Sciences, Physical Sciences, Engineering

1.   Consult the Subject Index and record the year and the
     citation number.

     Sample entry from the Subject Index of Conference
     Papers Index:

①   ②

Land Application/Treatment of Residue Produced in the 82-009826
Land Disposal of Hazardous Wastes, Current Research on..............82-008752
Land of the Hand, Delayed Primary Suture of Flexor Tendons 82-012203
Land Treated, The Fate of Mutagenic Compounds When Hazardous .82-008777
Land Treatment of Tannery Sludges, Field Evaluation on..............82-008779
Land Treatment of Waste as an Industrial Siting Advantage 82-009918

     1. subject   2. year, citation number
Reprinted with permission of Cambridge Scientific Abstracts.

2. Turn to the Citation Section, find the year and the
    citation number, and record the citation.

    Sample entry from the Citation Section of the Conference
    Papers Index:

(1) **821 5010: Eighth Annual Research Symposium Land Disposal,
    Incineration and Treatment of Hazardous Waste**

(2) 8-10 Mar 82

(3) Ft. Mitchell, KY

(4) Solid and Hazardous Waste Research Division and Industrial
    Pollution Control Division, Office Research and Development,
    U.S. Environmental Protection Agency

(5) ORDERING INFORMATION: Proceedings available: NTIS, De-
    partment of Commerce, 5285 Port Royal Rd., Springfield, VA
    22161; Order No. PB-82 173022; Paper copy $39.00 (A24); Fiche
    $4.00 (A01); Treatment & Incineration Section of Proceedings
    from L. Staley, IERL, EPA, Cincinnati, OH.

(6) **82-008752.** Current Research on Land Disposal of Hazardous Wastes. *N.B. Scho-
    maker, J.V. Klingshirn* (U.S. Environmental Protection Agency, Cincinnati, OH). (7)
    82-008753. Verification of the U.S. EPA HSSWDS Hydrologic Simulation Model.

    1. world meeting registry number, conference
    title 2. dates 3. location 4. sponsoring
    organization 5. ordering information 6. year,
    citation number, title of article, authors
    7. first author's address

Reprinted with permission of Cambridge Scientific Abstracts.

V. Directory of Published Proceedings.   Series SEMT.
    Science/Engineering/Medicine/Technology

The Directory of Published Proceedings began in 1964, and
appears monthly for ten months from September to June. The
Directory of Published Proceedings appears quarterly and
cumulates yearly. The Directory of Published Proceedings
indexes preprints and published proceedings which originate
from meetings, congresses, conferences, symposia, seminars,
and summer schools held all over the world.

Order of Search:

			Date/Number
Step 1.a.	Subject/Sponsor Index	Record:	5/78 - 3612
or b.	Editor Index	Record:	5/78 - 3612
or c.	Location Index	Record:	5/78 - 3612
Step 2.	Chronological Proceedings		
	Listing	Find:	5/78 - 3612
		Record:	citation

Procedure for Using the Subject/Sponsor Index of the
Directory of Published Proceedings

1. Consult the Subject/Sponsor Index and record the date
    and citation number.

    Sample entry from the Subject/Sponsor Index of the
    Directory of Published Proceedings:

    (1) Blood viscosity in heart disease, thromboembolism &
        cancer   5/78-3612 (2)

    1. subject   2. month, year, citation number

Reprinted with permission of the InterDok Corporation.

2. Turn to the Chronological Proceedings Listing, find the
    month, year and citation number and record the citation.

    Sample entry from the Chronological Proceedings Listing
    of the Directory of Published Proceedings:

    (1) 5/78
    (2) 3612   Sydney, N.S.W., Australia
               Blood viscosity in heart disease & cancer, Conf. on (3)
               Blood viscosity in heart disease, thromboembolism & (3)
               cancer
               (5) Pergamon Press (4)
               Ed: L. Dintenfass, & G. V. F. Seaman
               $40.00 1981 ISBN 0-08-024954-X 192p. (6)

    1. month, year   2. citation number, location
    3. title, conference title   4. publisher
    5. editor   6. price, year, International Standard
    Book Number, number of pages

Reprinted with permission of the InterDok Corporation.

VI. Index to Scientific & Technical Proceedings

The Index to Scientific & Technical Proceedings has monthly
issues and semiannual cumulations. This index includes proceedings published as books, reports, sets of preprints, or
parts of journals. Abstracts for meetings are not included.
The publications indexed are gathered from throughout the
world. The database for this index is ISI/ISTP&B. Further
information on this database may be found in Appendix III
under "Science, Technology and Agriculture."

Order of Search:

			Proceedings no./Page no.	
Step 1.a.	Permuterm Subject Index	Record:	P11997	11
or b.	Author/Editor Index	Record:	P11997	11
or c.	Category Index	Record:	P11997	
or d.	Sponsor Index	Record:	P11997	
or e.	Meeting Location Index	Record:	P11997	
or f.	Corporate Index	Record:	P11997	11
Step 2.	Contents of Proceedings	Find:	P11997	
		Record:	citation	

Procedure for Using the Permuterm Subject Index of the Index
to Scientific & Technical Proceedings

1. Consult the Permuterm Subject Index and record the
    proceedings number and the page number.

    Sample entry from the Permuterm Subject Index of the
    Index to Scientific & Technical Proceedings:

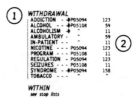

1. primary term   2. co-term, proceedings number,
page number

2. Turn to the Contents of Proceedings and find the abstract number and record the citation.

Sample entry from the Contents of Proceedings of the Index to Scientific & Technical Proceedings:

(1) P05108
(2) **9TH ANNUAL MEDICAL - SCIENTIFIC CONF OF THE NATIONAL ALCOHOLISM FORUM, St Louis, MO, May 1-3, 1978.**
(3) *Sponsors: Natl Council Alcoholism/ Amer Med Soc Alcoholism/ Res Soc Alcoholism*
(4) CURRENTS IN ALCOHOLISM, VOL 6: Treatment and Rehabilitation and Epidemiology
(5) Ed: M. GALANTER
(6) Grune & Stratton, New York, 1979, 345 pp., 33 chaps., $33.50 hardbound, LC# 76-30552, ISBN 0-8089-1201-1
(7) ACADEMIC PRESS 111 FIFTH AVE NEW YORK, NY 10003 (8)

(9) OVERVIEW OF TREATMENT AND REHABILITATION. *D.W. Goodwin* (Univ Kansas,Med Ctr,Dept Psychiat Kansas City KS 66103) 1
ALCOHOLIC IN THE GENERAL-HOSPITAL - INTRODUCTION. *J. Solomon* (Suny Downstate Med-Ctr Brooklyn NY 11203) 7
WITHDRAWAL SEIZURES IN AN IN-PATIENT ALCOHOLISM PROGRAM. *J.A. Newsom* (S Coast Community Hosp,Careunit Laguna CA) 11 (10)
INPATIENT REHABILITATION FOR THE MEDICALLY ILL ALCOHOLIC. *M. Galanter, J. Schubmehl, H.N. Adel, S.C. Sofer* (Yeshiva Univ Albert Einstein Coll Med,Dept Psychiat Bronx NY 10461) 15
RELIABLE INTERPRETATION OF THE NCA CRITERIA IN AN ESTIMATE OF THE PREVALENCE OF ALCOHOLISM IN A GENERAL-HOSPITAL. *R.G.M. Johnston, D.G. Mayfield, B.W. Lex* (Providence Vet Adm Hosp,Med Ctr,Dept Psychiat Providence RI) 25
ALCOHOLISM IN A GENERAL-HOSPITAL POPULATION. *N. Decker, W.E. Fann, P. Girardin, D.H. Miller, T. Kanas* (Vet Adm Hosp,Med Ctr,Dept Psychiat Houston TX 77211) 33
CURRENT PERSPECTIVES ON THE RECOVERING ALCOHOLIC IN AMBULATORY TREATMENT - INTRODUCTION. *G.R. Jacobson* (De Paul Rehabil Hosp,Dept Res Evaluat & Training Milwaukee WI) 41
NORMAL RECOVERY SYMPTOMS FREQUENTLY EXPERIENCED BY THE RECOVERING ALCOHOLIC. *J.E. Massman* (USN,Med Corps,Fpo Seattle WA) 51
AMBULATORY ALCOHOL WITHDRAWAL. *F.S. Tennant* (Univ Calif Los Angeles,Sch Publ Hlth,Ctr Hlth Sci,Div Epidemiol Los Angeles CA 90024) 59
STUDENT COUNSELOR ATTITUDES AND HOW THEY AFFECT CLIENTS - EXPRESSED NEGATIVITY IS HELPFUL. *R.E. Worden* (Univ Calif Los Angeles,Dept Psychiat Los Angeles CA 90024) 63
RELIGIOUS CONVERSION - EXPERIMENTAL-MODEL FOR AFFECTING ALCOHOLIC DENIAL. *M. Galanter* 69
PSYCHOTHERAPY AND THE MEMBER OF ALCOHOLICS ANONYMOUS. *J. Kinney, M. Montgomery* (Dartmouth Coll,Sch Med,Dept Psychiat Hanover NH 03755) 79
EVALUATION AND OUTCOME - INTRODUCTION. *K.A. Keeley* (New York State Div Substance Abuse Serv,Med Serv New York NY) 87
FOLLOW-UP-STUDY OF ALCOHOLICS AT 6, 12 AND 24 MONTHS. *E. Gottheil, C.C. Thornton, T.E. Skoloda, A.I. Alterman* (Thomas Jefferson Univ,Dept Psychiat & Behav Sci Philadelphia PA 19107) 91
TOWARD A SYSTEM FOR PREDICTION OF POST-TREATMENT ABSTINENCE AND ADAPTATION. *M.L. Kammeier, J.J. Conley* (Hazelden Fdn Ctr City MN) 111
EVALUATION OF A TREATMENT PROGRAM FOR DRUNK DRIVING OFFENDERS. *E.W. Fine, R.A. Steer, P.E. Scoles* (Albert Einstein Med Ctr,Program Addict Dis Philadelphia PA 19141) 121

1. proceedings number 2. conference title, location, date 3. sponsors 4. book title with volume 5. editor 6. publisher, address, date, pages, chapters, price, Library of Congress number 7. International Standard Book Number 8. order address 9. title of article, author 10. address of author

Finding Research Done By Doctoral Candidates

Dissertations (published results of doctoral research), are not always included in the abstracts and indexes discussed in Chapter 5. It is necessary, therefore, to search the indexes and abstracts which are specifically for dissertations, Dissertation Abstracts International and Comprehensive Dissertation Index.

The research done by a doctoral candidate may be published in a journal or book in addition to the dissertation. The more important the doctoral research, the better chance that it will be published elsewhere. For this reason, it may not be necessary to search for dissertations. If, however, one is seeking all the pertinent literature on a topic or looking for a topic that no one else has apparently researched, it is appropriate to search for dissertations.

VII. Comprehensive Dissertation Index

Comprehensive Dissertation Index lists virtually all doctoral dissertations produced in North America since 1861 when the first doctorates were granted. The original volumes cover the span between 1961 and 1972. After 1972 the indexes are issued yearly. Comprehensive Dissertation Index is a companion series to Dissertation Abstracts International, and also serves as an index to Dissertation Abstracts International. The contents of these items are combined in the database COMPREHENSIVE DISSERTATION INDEX or DISSERTATION ABSTRACTS (depending on the vendor). Further information on this database may be found in Appendix III under "Science, Technology and Agriculture."

Order of Search:

			Volume	Issue	Series	Page
Step 1.a.	Keyword Index	Record:	40	10	B	4961
or b.	Author Index	Record:	40	10	B	4961
Step 2.	Abstracts found in Dissertation Abstracts					
	International	Find:	40	10	B	4961
		Record:	citation			

Procedure for Using Comprehensive Dissertation Index

Consult the index for the subject and record the citation.

Sample entry from the index of Comprehensive Dissertation Index:

(1) WIND-POWERED
AN IMPROVED CONTROL STRATEGY FOR WIND-
POWERED REFRIGERATED STORAGE OF APPLES.— (2)
(3) BALDWIN, JOHN DEROUET COUPER (PH.D. 1979
VIRGINIA POLYTECHNIC INSTITUTE AND STATE
UNIVERSITY) 168p. 40/10B, p.4911 DEM80–07330 (4)

WIND-PRODUCED
RAPID-SCANNING MEASUREMENTS OF WIND-
PRODUCED DOPPLER ON AN ASYMMETRICAL
MICROWAVE TRANSHORIZON PROPAGATION PATH.—
FLEMING, RONALD DOUGLAS (PH.D. 1979 STANFORD
UNIVERSITY) 131p. 40/07B, p.3302 DEM80–01917

1. subject   2. title of dissertation   3. author,
degree, degree date, university awarding degree
4. number of pages, *DAI volume, DAI issue,
DAI series, DAI page, order number

*DAI is Dissertation Abstracts International

VIII.   Dissertation Abstracts International. B. Science
and Engineering

Dissertation Abstracts International consists of abstracts of
doctoral dissertations submitted to University Microfilms by
430 institutions in the United States and Canada. Dissertation Abstracts International appears monthly with yearly
cumulations. Its contents and the contents of Comprehensive
Dissertation Index from 1861 forward form the database called
COMPREHENSIVE DISSERTATION INDEX or DISSERTATION ABSTRACTS.
Further information on this database may be found in
Appendix III under "Science, Technology and Agriculture."

Order of Search:

			Volume/Issue/Page/Series			
Step 1.a.	Keyword Title Index	Record:			p.4292	– B
or b.	Author Index	Record:	42	11	p.4292	– B
Step 2.	Abstracts	Find:	42	11	p.4292	– B
		Record:	citation			

Procedure for Using the Keyword Title Index of Dissertation
Abstracts International.   B.   Science and Engineering

1.   Consult the Subject Index and record the abstract number.

Sample entry from the Keyword Title Index of Dissertation
Abstracts International:

① **SNAKES**
DERMAL IRIDOPHORES IN SNAKES; CORRELATIONS
WITH HABITAT ADAPTATION AND PHYLOGENY
(ANATOMY) KLEESE, WILLIAM CARL, p.4272–B
② THERMAL AND SPATIAL ECOLOGY OF THREE SPECIES
OF WATER SNAKES (NERODIA) IN A LOUISIANA
SWAMP (ECOLOGY) MICHOT, THOMAS CLAUD,   ③
④ p.4292–B

SN1
ISOLATION AND CHARACTERIZATION OF THE MODIFIED
BASE FOUND FOR BACTERIOPHAGE SN1 DNA
(MICROBIOLOGY) RICE, WILLIAM CLINTON, p.4310–B

SOBER
THE AGGRESSIVE INTERACTIONS OF INTOXICATED AND
SOBER DYADS (PSYCHOLOGY, CLINICAL) LEONARD,
KENNETH EARL, p.4581–B

SOCIAL
A STUDY OF PARAPROFESSIONAL AND PROFESSIONAL
SOCIAL INFLUENCE ON SELF-EFFICACY
EXPECTATIONS (PSYCHOLOGY, SOCIAL) JENNINGS,
MARTHA LEE, p.4619–B
ALTERNATIVE REPRODUCTIVE TACTICS OF SINGLE
FOUNDRESSES OF A SOCIAL WASP, POLISTES
FUSCATUS (ZOOLOGY) KLAHN, JEFFREY EUGENE,
p.4324–B
ANALYSIS OF INTERPERSONAL SOCIAL SKILLS IN
DELINQUENT AND NONDELINQUENT ADOLESCENT
BOYS (PSYCHOLOGY, CLINICAL) GREEN, CORNELIA
ANN, p.4577–B
CHILDREN'S REWARD ALLOCATIONS: THE INFLUENCE
OF UNDERSTANDING PROPORTIONALITY, PHYSICAL-
PERCEPTUAL PERSPECTIVE-TAKING, AND COGNITIVE-
SOCIAL PERSPECTIVE-TAKING (PSYCHOLOGY,
GENERAL) TOMPKINS, BRIGITTE MEGGLE, p.4564–B
CHILDREN'S UNDERSTANDING OF PEER BEHAVIOR:
VARIATIONS AS A FUNCTION OF AFFECT, AGE, SOCIAL
STATUS AND SEX OF PERCEIVER (PSYCHOLOGY,
SOCIAL) HYMEL, SHELLEY CLAIRE, p.4619–B
COMMUNICATIVE COMPETENCY IN MIDDLE CHILDHOOD:
AN ANALYSIS OF THE SOCIAL DISCOURSE OF
POPULAR AND REJECTED THIRD AND SIXTH GRADE
CHILDREN (PSYCHOLOGY, SOCIAL) AUSTIN, ANN
MARIE BERGHOUT, p.4615–B
CONTROL OF ARRIVALS TO A GI/M/1/LIFO QUEUEING
SYSTEM: INDIVIDUAL AND SOCIAL OPTIMIZATION
(OPERATIONS RESEARCH) WALTHER, ELEANOR ANN,
p.4554–B
COPING STRATEGIES, SOCIAL SUPPORT, AND ROLE
RELATED PROBLEMS AS PREDICTORS OF BURNOUT IN
NURSES (PSYCHOLOGY, SOCIAL) KIMMEL, MARK
REYE, p.4621–B

   1. subject   2. title   3. author   4. page, series

2.   Turn to the abstracts section and find the abstract
     number and record the citation.

     Sample entry from the Abstracts section of Dissertation
     Abstracts International:

(1) **THERMAL AND SPATIAL ECOLOGY OF THREE SPECIES OF WATER SNAKES (*NERODIA*) IN A LOUISIANA SWAMP**
                                    Order No. DA8207833 (2)
(3) MICHOT, THOMAS CLAUD, PH.D. *The Louisiana State University and Agricultural and Mechanical Col.*, 1981. 158pp. Supervisor: (4)
(5) Professor Henry R. Mushinsky

Biotelemetry was used to study thermal and spatial relationships in *Nerodia fasciata confluens, N. c. cyclopion*, and *N. r. rhombifera*. Twenty snakes were monitored between April 1978 and September 1979 in Ascension Parish, Louisiana. Laboratory-determined preferred temperature ranges were compared to environmental temperatures from air, soil, and water to predict thermally optimum microhabitats. Comparison of observed and predicted microhabitats for each observation showed that *N. fasciata* was found more frequently in the thermally optimum microhabitat than were *N. cyclopion* and *N. rhombifera*. *Nerodia cyclopion* consistently showed thermal nonconformity by altering the relationship between body (BT) and ambient (AT) temperatures so that BT was closer to the preferred range when AT was high or low. All species showed the highest degree of thermoregulation in spring/fall; the lowest degree of thermoregulation was found in summer for *N. cyclopion*, and in winter for the other two species. Snake movements showed a high degree of variation. Snakes typically stayed in a home area for about 20 days before making a major movement (> 100 m). *Nerodia fasciata* moved significantly more than *N. rhombifera*. The latter species stayed closer to land, spent more time underground, and, when in water, was found at greater depths than the other two species. The mean home range polygon for all observations was 5.96 ha, with values ranging from 0.03 to 15.39 ha. Home range size showed much variation and was not significantly correlated with species, sex, reproductive condition, weight, time of year, length of tracking period or interval between observations.

     1. title of dissertation   2. order number
     3. author, degree, degree granting institution
     4. year, number of pages   5. supervisor or
     major professor

7
Locating the Abstracts and Indexes for Government Documents

Introduction

The United States Government is the largest publisher in the world, and publishes materials on many scientific topics. Its publications range from pamphlets on how to plant a garden to highly technical research papers, lengthy books, and statistical publications. In libraries, these publications are often arranged by government agencies and departments rather than by subject. It is therefore desirable to gain a familiarity with the departments and to learn to use indexes for government documents. Technical reports which document government sponsored research are indexed in such publications as <u>Scientific and Technical Aerospace Reports</u> and <u>Government Reports Announcements & Index</u>. State governments issue a variety of publications, many of which are indexed in the <u>Monthly Checklist of State Publications</u>. Agricultural Experiment Station and Agricultural Extension Service publications have no central index which is complete; they may be listed with other state publications in the <u>Monthly Checklist of State Publications</u> or in other indexes.

United States Government Department and Agency Publications

Of particular importance to persons interested in science and technology are those publications of the Agriculture Department, the National Bureau of Standards, the Patent and Trademark Office, National Oceanic and Atmospheric Administration, Census Bureau, Public Health Service, Interior Department, Nuclear Regulatory Commission, Environmental Protection Agency, National Aeronautics and Space Administration, Energy Department, National Science Foundation, and the Smithsonian Institution. These bodies issue reports, yearbooks, journals, indexes, statistics, and studies, which provide access by the public to research and development in the United States and to some extent in other areas of the world.

Documents are often arranged according to their issuing body,
by a system of classification based on the Government Printing
Office classification number, otherwise known as the Superintendent of Documents number. Usually the first letter or
letters match the beginning letters of the issuing organization. For example, "A" is the letter for the Agriculture
Department and "NS" is the indication for the National Science
Foundation. This is called the "author symbol." Following
the author symbol is a number. If the number is "1" then the
publication is by the parent organization; if it is "2" or
greater, it is by a subordinate bureau or office.

A 1	Agriculture Department
A 77	Agricultural Research Service

A period sets off the organization from the series number.
The series number is derived from a list such as that which
follows:

.1:	Annual Report
.2:	General Publications
.3:	Bulletins
.4:	Circulars

Putting these letters and numbers together forms the "class
stem." The following is an example:

A 77.2	Class stem for a general publication of the Agricultural Research Service

The "book number" (after the colon) follows the "class stem."
Sometimes this number is the last three digits in the year;
thus "1976" would be "976." In some other cases the Cutter
number (number used after the decimal in the Library of
Congress number or the Dewey number) is used as the "book
number."

I. Monthly Catalog of United States Government Publications

The Monthly Catalog is the main index to federal documents.
Generally, this index provides access to United States government documents which are not classified or reports of government sponsored research. Published by the Superintendent of
Documents, it includes items available for sale from the
Government Printing Office and other issuing offices.
Entries conform to Anglo-American cataloging rules and
utilize Library of Congress subject headings. Each month
the catalog consists of the entries arranged by agencies,
an author index, title index, subject index, series/report
index, stock number index, and title key word index. A
machine readable database, the GPO MONTHLY CATALOG, exists
for this index; further information on this database may be
found in Appendix III under "Government Documents, United
States."

Order of Search:

		Year/Entry no./GPO cat. no.
Step 1.a.	Author Index	Record: 81-5504
or b.	Title Index	Record: 81-5504
or c.	Subject Index	Record: 81-5504
or d.	Series/ Report Index	Record: 81-5504
Step 2.	Citation or entry	Find: 81-5504 Record: E1.26:40174-01

Procedure for Using the Monthly Catalog of United States Government Publications

1. Consult the subject index and record the entry number.

    Sample entry from the subject index of the Monthly Catalog of United States Government Publications:

Energy conservation — United States.

(1) Ceramic heat recuperators for industrial heat recovery : interim technical report

(2) /,   81-5504

Community and State Energy Planning Assistance Act of 1980 : report together with minority views (to accompany H.R. 7945) (including cost estimate of the Congressional Budget Office).,   81-883

Cutting energy costs.,   81-5383

Delays and uncertain energy savings in program to promote state energy conservation : report to the Congress /, 81-387

DOD energy monitoring and control systems—potential for nonenergy savings—better planning and guidance needed : report to the Secretary of Defense /,   81-487

1. subject   2. entry number

2. Turn to the citation section, find the entry number, and record the citation.

Sample entry from the citation section of the <u>Monthly Catalog of United States Government Publications</u>:

(1) **81-5504**
                                    E 1.26:40174-01 (2)
(3) Ceramic heat recuperators for industrial heat recovery : interim
        technical report / prepared by GTE Products Corporation (4)
        and PAR Enterprises, Inc. ; prepared for U.S. Department of
        Energy, Assistant Secretary Conservation and Solar Energy,
        Office of Industrial Programs. — Washington, D.C. : The
(5) Office : For sale by the Supt. of Docs., U.S. G.P.O. ; Spring-
        field, Va. (5285 Port Royal Rd., Springfield, Va., 22161) :
        Available from National Technical Information Service, 1980.
           xvii, 129 p. : ill. ; 28 cm. (6)
(7)   "May 1980."
         Includes bibliographical references.
(8)   "DOE/CS/40174-01."
         "Contract no. AC01-76CS40174." (9)
(10)   ●Item 429-T-2
         S/N 061-000-00469-6 @ GPO   (11)
(12) $5.00
           1. Energy conservation — United States.   2. Heat recovery. (13)
           3. Ceramic materials. I. United States. Dept. of Energy.
(14)   Assistant Secretary for Conservation and Solar Energy.
         Office of Industrial Programs. II. GTE Products Corpora-
         tion. III. PAR Enterprises.
(15)   OCLC 7374159

1. entry number   2. Superintendent of Documents
classification number   3. title   4. issuing
agencies   5. order information   6. physical
description   7. notes   8. document number
9. contract number   10. depository item symbol
and item number   11. stock number   12. price
13. subject headings   14. added entries
15. OCLC number

II. The Cumulative Subject Index to the Monthly Catalog of
     United States Government Publications, 1900-1971

This is the most important of several cumulative indexes for
the Monthly Catalog. Its fifteen volume set merged forty-
eight annual indexes, two decennial indexes, and one half
year index into one single-alphabet subject index and added
original indexing of some early issues.

Order of Search:

	Page or Year/entry no. /	GPO cat. no.
Step 1. Subject Index (Cum. Subj. Index Monthly Catalog)	Record: (38) 1520	
Step 2. Monthly Catalog citations	Find: 1938 1520	Record: A61.10:12

Procedure for Using the Cumulative Subject Index of the
Monthly Catalog of United States Government Publications

1. Consult the subject index and record year and entry
    number.

    Sample entry from the subject index of the Cumulative
    Subject Index of the Monthly Catalog of United States
    Government Publications:

        (1) farm -
                 and village families (38) 1520 (2)
                 families -
                     cost-price squeeze (53) 19581, 19609-610
                     electricity (52) 14498
                     expenditures, 1955, surveys (58) 6454; (60) 1406
                     in Livingston Co., N.Y. (24) 338
                     outlook (talks) (53) 20237; (55) 3792
                     references (58) 94
                   , trends and patterns (58) 2775
                 loans for better living (51) 4263; (52) 36

    1. subject   2. year, page

2. Turn to the citation section of the <u>Monthly Catalog</u>,
    find the year and entry number, and record the citation.

Sample entry from the citation section of the <u>Monthly
Catalog of United States Public Documents</u>:

(1) 1520   DECEMBER 1938

                    FARM SECURITY ADMINISTRATION (2)

(3) *Family living.* Standard of living of farm and village families in 6 South Dakota (4)
    counties, 1935; [by] W. F. Kumlien, Charles P. Loomis, Zetta E. Bankert,
    Edmund deS. Brunner [and] Robert L. MacNamara. n. p., Mar. 1938. 63 p. il. (5)
(6) (Social research report 12; [South Dakota Agricultural Experiment Station]
    Bulletin 320.) [South Dakota Agricultural Experiment Station cooperating
(7) with Works Progress Administration, Farm Security Administration, and
    Agricultural Economics Bureau.] †   A 61.10: 12 (8)
(9)   NOTE.—This report was published by the South Dakota Agricultural Experiment
    Station as Bulletin 320. The Farm Security Administration has incorporated this
    publication into their Social research report series as no. 12, by pasting a tab entitled
    Social research report no. 12, at head of title.

1. page, date   2. agency   3. title   4. authors
5. imprint, physical description   6. series
statement   7. agencies associated with the
document   8. Superintendent of Documents
classification number   9. note

                    Specialized Document Indexes

I.   American Statistics Index

The <u>American Statistics Index</u> (ASI), published by Congressional Information Service (CIS) since 1974, is a master
guide index and abstract service for the statistical publications of the United States Government. The service strives
to acquire statistical publications comprehensively, including
items not listed in the <u>Monthly Catalog</u> or available in
depository libraries. All publications can be ordered
directly from CIS. Monthly and annual indexes are issued.
A machine readable database, ASI, exists for this index;
further information on this database may be found in
Appendix III under "Government Documents, United States."

Order of Search:

	ASI accession no./	GPO cat. no.
Step 1.a. Index of Subject Names	Record: 1612-1	
or b. Index by Categories Geographic Breakdown	Record: 1612-1	
Economic Breakdown	Record: 1612-1	
Demographic Breakdown	Record: 1612-1	
or c. Index by Titles	Record: 1612-1	
or d. Index by Agency Report No.	Record: 1612-1	
Step 2 Abstracts	Find: 1612-1	Record: A105.10

Procedure for Using the American Statistics Index

1. Consult the Index by Subjects and Names and record the ASI accession number.

   Sample entry from the Index by Subjects and Names of the American Statistics Index:

   (1) **Agricultural exports and imports**
        Agricultural outlook, 1979, annual conf
        papers, -25164-1.1
   (2) *Agricultural Situation,* monthly crop
        reporters magazine, 1612-1   (3)
        Agricultural Stabilization and Conservation
        Service commodity programs, 1979 annual
        commodity fact sheet series, 1806-4
        Agriculture chartbook on general farm
        production, marketing, and trade trends,
        food consumption, and food and nutrition
        programs, 1960s-79 and earlier, annual
        rpt, 1504-3
        Business statistics, detailed data for major
        industries and economic indicators,
        Survey of Current Business monthly rpt,
        2702-1.12

   1. subject   2. title   3. ASI accession number

American Statistics Index Annual, 1979.
Congressional Information Service, Inc.
4520 East-West Highway, Bethesda, MD 20814
Reprinted with permission.

2. Turn to the Abstracts section, find the ASI accession number, and record the citation.

    Sample entry from the Abstracts section of the <u>American Statistics Index</u>:

1612   (ESCS)
① **CROP REPORTING BOARD: GENERAL**
Current Periodicals

---

② **1612-1**   **AGRICULTURAL SITUATION,** ③
                  The Crop Reporters
                  Magazine
          ④ 11 issues yearly.
              Approx. 15 p. ●Item 19. ⑤
          ⑥ GPO: $7.75 per yr.; single
              copies avail. from issuing
              agency at no charge.
              ASI/MF/3
              S/N 001-028-80001-1.
          ⑦ *A105.10:(v.nos.&nos.)
              MC 79-128. LC Agr 26-1797. ⑧

⑨ Monthly journal containing topical articles of general agricultural interest to farmers and ranchers. Distributed free to all crop and livestock reporters.

Each issue contains 5-8 short articles, often with some text statistics, and the following regular features:

a. Briefings. Synopses of recent reports of economic, marketing, and research developments affecting farmers.

b. Statistical barometer. Table presenting latest available data on agricultural prices, farm income and expenses, and agricultural trade.

Data for Jan./Feb. are combined in a single issue.
Issues covered during 1979: Nov. 1978-Sept. 1979 (P) (Vol. 62, Nos. 10, 11; Vol. 63, Nos. 1-8); filmed quarterly.

---

1. agency   2. ASI accession number   3. title of journal   4. frequency   5. number of pages, depository item number   6. hardcopy availability information   7. Superintendent of Documents classification number   8. GPO Monthly Catalog entry number, Library of Congress card number   9. annotation

II.   CIS/Index to Publications of the United States Congress

The CIS/Index to Publications of the United States Congress
is a monthly indexing and abstracting service from Congressional Information Service (CIS). CIS provides a more
detailed index to congressional documents than exists in the
Monthly Catalog and makes the documents themselves available
for purchase. Annual and multiple year indexes are available
since 1970. The Congressional Record is not included. A
machine readable database, CIS, exists for this index; further
information on this database may be found in Appendix III
under "Government Documents, United States."

Order of Search:

		CIS accession no./	GPO cat. no.
Step 1.a.	Index of Sub- ject & Names	Record: H501.3	
or b.	Index of Titles	Record: H501.3	
or c.	Index of Bills	Record: H501.3	
or d.	Index of Report Numbers	Record: H501.3	
or e.	Index of Docu- ment Numbers	Record: H501.3	
or f.	Index of Com- mittee & Sub- committee Chairmen	Record: H440	
Step 2	Abstracts	Find: H501.3 or H440	Record: Y4In8/496-169

Procedure for Using the CIS/Annual

1. Consult the Index of Subject and Names and record the
    CIS accession number.

    Sample entry from the Index of Subject and Names of the
    CIS Annual:

(1) **Animal feed and forage**
     Agric outlook, 1980 USDA conf papers,
     S162-1
     Antibiotics in animal feed, restriction,
     H501-3
     (2)

    1. subject   2. CIS accession number

CIS/Index 1981 Congressional Information
Service, Inc. 4520 East-West Highway,
Bethesda, MD 20814
Reprinted with permission.

2. Turn to the Abstracts section, find the CIS accession
    number, and record the citation.

    Sample entry from the Abstracts section of the CIS Annual:

(1) H501–3   ANTIBIOTICS IN ANIMAL (2)
              FEED.
       (3) June 12, 24, 1980. 96-2.
       (5) iv+623 p. † CIS/MF/9 (4)
       (5) •Item 1019.
              °Y4.In8/4:96-169. (6)
       (7) MC 81-2019. LC 80-603463.
(8) Committee Serial No. 96-169. Hearings before
    the *Subcom on Health and the Environment* to
    consider H.R. 7285 (text, p. 3-6), the Antibiotics
    Preservation Act, to amend the Federal Food,
    Drug, and Cosmetic Act to authorize FDA to
    restrict the use of subtherapeutic doses of antibi-
    otics in livestock feed.
        Focuses on concern that continued farm use of
    antibiotics may foster spread of resistant bacteria
    and lessen human effectiveness of antibiotic
    treatment.
        Supplementary material (p. 482-623) includes
    submitted statements, correspondence, and
    "Economic Impact Study: Effects of a Prohibi-
    tion on the Use of Selected Animal Drugs,"
    Chase Econometric Associates report prepared
    for American Cyanamid et al., Oct. 1979, with
    tables, graphs (p. 581-623).

(9) H501–3.1: June 12, 1980. p. 7-308.
    Witness: DINGELL, John D., (Rep, D-Mich) (10)
(11) *Statement and Discussion:* Review of human
    health risks related to antibiotic use in animal
    feed (related articles, p. 17-305); importance
    of H.R. 7285.

1. CIS accession number for series   2. title of
publication   3. date, Congress and session
4. collation, microfiche availability and unit
count   5. Superintendent of Documents item number
6. Superintendent of Documents classification
number   7. GPO Monthly Catalog entry number,
Library of Congress card number   8. annotation
for series   9. CIS accession number for individual
testimony, date of testimony, pages   10. name and
affiliation of witness   11. summary of testimony

III. Government Reports Announcements & Index

The National Technical Information Service (NTIS) publishes
Government Reports Announcements & Index every two weeks.
It is an index and abstracting service for unclassified
United States Government sponsored research, development and
engineering reports. NTIS also sells the reports and provides a machine readable database called NTIS; further
information on this database may be found in Appendix III
under "Science and Technology." Some of the agencies which
contribute reports are the Department of Defense, National
Aeronautics and Space Administration, Department of Energy,
Department of Commerce, and other government agencies, as
well as local and foreign units.

Order of Search:

			Year/Issue/Page/	Order no.
Government Reports Index				
Step 1.a. Keyword Index	Record:	81 - 10	1963	PB81-144651
or b. Personal Author	Record:	81 - 10	1963	PB81-144651
or c. Corporate Author	Record:	81 - 10	1963	PB81-144651
or d. Contract/Grant				
No. Index	Record:	81 - 10	1963	PB81-144651
or e. NTIS Order/				
Report No.	Record:	81 - 10	1963	PB81-144651
Government Reports Announcements				
Step 2 Abstracts	Find:	81 - 10	1963	PB81-144651
	Record:	citation		

Procedure for Using the Government Reports Announcements &
Index

1. Consult the Keyword Index and record the page number.

Sample entry from the Keyword Index of the Government
Reports Annual Index:

① DRIP IRRIGATION
   Treatment of Mililani STP Effluent for Drip Irrigation of Sug-
   arcane.
   PB81-144651   81-10 1963 PC **A03**/MF **A01** ②

1. subject   2. order number, year, issue,
page, price codes

2.   Turn to the Abstracts section, find the page number, order number, and record the citation.

Sample entry from the Abstracts section of the Government Reports Announcements:

(1) **PB81-144651**   PC **A03**/MF **A01**
Hawaii Univ., Honolulu. Water Resources Re- (2)
search Center.
(3) **Treatment of Mililani STP Effluent for Drip Irrigation of Sugarcane.**
Technical rept. Oct 76-Oct 78,
Edward K. F. Liu, and Reginald H. F. Young. Jul (4)
(5) 79, 40p TR-128, W81-00984
Contract DI-14-34-0001-9013 (6)

(7) Reclaimed municipal waste water effluent is intended for use as irrigation water, primarily on sugarcane, the largest single user of water in the state.
Various studies have found that, with proper irrigation management, sugar yields can increase when
sewage effluent is used in conjunction with normal
irrigation ditch water. The objective of an ongoing
study by the WRRC is to determine the feasibility
of using secondary sewage effluent in drip irrigation. The sewage effluent selected for reclamation
studies comes from the Mililani Sewage Treatment
Plant (STP) which is ideally suited for reclamation
and reuse of its effluent. The objective of this study
was to investigate the feasibility of various treatment methods for decreasing the concentration of
suspended solids in the effluent discharged by the
Mililani STP. The level of suspended solids in
Waiahole Ditch water and in the Mililani STP effluent was established, and the method was determined of treatment required at Mililani STP to
ensure the same concentration of suspended
solids in the discharged effluent as in Waiahole
Ditch water. The treatment methods investigated
included chemical coagulation, granular media fil-
tration, and dissolved air flotation.

1. order number, availability/price codes
2. corporate or performing organization
3. report title   4. personal authors,
report date   5. page count, report numbers
6. contract or grant number   7. abstract

IV. Index to U.S. Government Periodicals

The Index to U.S. Government Periodicals, published by
Infordata International Incorporated since 1970, is a guide
to 172 titles by author and subject.   Titles which have sub-
stantive articles of research value are selected for inclusion.   Topics include agriculture, energy, medicine, military
science and engineering.   The index appears quarterly with
annual cumulations.

Order of Search:

Step 1. Subject & Author Index	Record: citation

Procedure for Using the Index to U.S. Government Periodicals

Consult the index for the subject and record the citation.
(Note Superintendent of Documents numbers of periodicals
inside front cover.)

Sample entry from the Index to U.S. Government
Periodicals:

(1) CELLS (2)
(3) Chromosome banding techniques. Digamber S.
     Borgaonkar and Raymond C. Lewandowski, ref
     Psychopharm Bul 16 1 60-61 Ja 80-091 (4)
Chromosome fragility in New Zealand Black mice:
     effect of ultraviolet and gamma radiations on fetal
     fibroblasts in vitro. A. Lakshma Reddy and Philip J.
     Fialkow, ref, gr J Nat Cancer Inst 64 4 939-941 Ap
     80-060
Cloning of Russet Burbank. Peter Gwynne, il, ch
     Mosaic 11 3 33-38 My-Je 80-071
Electrostatic charge plants. Stephen M. Berberich, il
     Agric Res 28 5 10-11 N 79-004

1. subject   2. title of article   3. authors,
special features   4. periodical information
(abbreviation of periodical title, volume,
issue, pages, date, microfiche order number)

V. Monthly Checklist of State Publications

Administrative entities of state government publish documents
which reflect the wide range of their interests: law enforce-
ment, agriculture, environment, education, highways, labor,
mental health, welfare, and vital statistics. Often
libraries which collect federal documents will also collect
documents for the state in which they are located. Access
to state documents is inconsistent, because in some states
there are systematic listings of the publications, and in
others there are not. Selected state materials may be
located by using the Monthly Checklist.

The Monthly Checklist of State Publications is a record of
state documents received by the Library of Congress. The
types of materials indexed may include periodicals, monographic series, statistical reports, official university
reports, agricultural documents, and publications of state
officials. The Library of Congress attempts to include all
state publications with a few exceptions (such as college
catalogs); for inclusion, it depends upon donations of the
items from state agencies. Cumulations appear annually.

Order of Search:

		Citation no.
Step 1. Index	Record:	19730
Step 2. Citation	Find:	19730
	Record:	citation

Procedure for Using the Monthly Checklist of State
Publications

1. Consult the index and record the citation number.

    Sample entry from the index of the Monthly Checklist:

(1) **Agricultural chemicals,** 16932 *see also*
     Insecticides; Pesticides
     —handbooks, manuals, etc.
     — —North Carolina, 19730 (2)

1. subject   2. citation number

2. Turn to the citation section, find the citation number, and record the citation.

    Sample entry from the citation section of the Monthly Checklist:

① - 19730 -
② NORTH CAROLINA STATE UNIVERSITY AT RALEIGH.
    School of Agriculture and Life Sciences.   North Caro-
    lina agricultural chemicals manual.   1977-78.   [Ra-   ③
    leigh]   2 v.   ill.   annual.   ④
    ⑤ $3. 50 a copy.   59-62888   ⑥

1. citation number 2. issuing agency 3. title, date, city 4. physical description and frequency 5. price 6. Library of Congress card number

VI.   Scientific and Technical Aerospace Reports

Scientific and Technical Aerospace Reports (STAR), produced by the National Aeronautics and Space Administration since 1963, is an index and abstracting service for scientific and technical publications which are related to aeronautics and space research and development. It appears semimonthly and includes NASA, NASA contracted, and other reports in aero-space disciplines from public and private agencies. Cumulations appear semiannually and annually.

Order of Search:

			NASA
			Issue/Page/accession no.
Step 1.a.	Subject Index	Record: 01 p0095	N80-10696
or b.	Personal Author Index	Record: 01 p0095	N80-10696
or c.	Corporate Source		
	Index	Record: 01 p0095	N80-10696
or d.	Contract Number Index	Record: 01 p0095	N80-10696
or e.	Report/Accession No.		
	Index	Record: 01 p0095	N80-10696
Step 2.	Abstracts	Find: 01 95	N80-10696
		Record: citation	

Procedure for Using the Scientific and Technical Aerospace Reports

1. Consult the Subject Index and record the NASA accession number.

    Sample entry from the Subject Index of the Scientific and Technical Aerospace Reports:

> (1) **EXHAUST EMISSION**
>   Emission assessment of conventional stationary
>   combustion systems. Volume 2: Internal combustion (2)
>   sources
>   (3) [PB-296390/8]   01   p0095   N80-10696

1. subject heading 2. title 3. report number, issue and page, NASA accession number

2. Turn to the abstracts section, find the NASA accession number, and record the citation.

    Sample entry from the abstracts section of the Scientific and Technical Aerospace Reports:

> (1) **N80-10696#** TRW, Inc., Redondo Beach, Calif.
>   **EMISSION ASSESSMENT OF CONVENTIONAL STATION-** (2)
>   **ARY COMBUSTION SYSTEMS. VOLUME 2: INTERNAL**
>   **COMBUSTION SOURCES** Final Report, Sep. 1976 - Jan.
>   **1979**
>   (3) C. C. Shih, J. W. Hammersma, D. G. Ackerman, R. G. Beimer,
>   M. L. Kraft, and M. M. Yamada Jan. 1979 239 p refs (4)
>   (5) (Contract EPA-68-02-2197)
>   (PB-296390/8;   EPA-600/7-79-029c)   Avail: NTIS (6)
>   HC A11/MF A01 CSCL 13B   (7)
>   (8)   Emissions from gas- and oil-fueled gas turbines and reciproca-
>   ting engines for electricity generation and industrial applications
>   are assessed. The results indicate that internal combustion sources
>   contribute significantly to the national emissions burden. The
>   source severity factor, defined as the ratio of the calculated
>   maximum ground level concentration of the pollutant species to
>   the level at which a potential environmental hazard exists, was
>   used to identify pollutants of environmental concern.   GRA

1. NASA accession number, corporate source 2. title
3. authors 4. date, number of pages, references
5. contract 6. report number, availability source
7. COSATI code 8. abstract

Agricultural Experiment Station and Extension Service Publications

The United States Agricultural Experiment Stations began about a century ago. The purpose of the Stations is to improve the states' agriculture by conducting research and promulgating the results through Extension Service Offices. Publications vary from serials and monographs on scientific research to pamphlets for the lay person. The public may obtain these at Extension Service Offices or in libraries, where they may be in a separate collection of their own, mixed in with the rest of the library's collection, or shelved with state documents. There is no index for all of the publications, so libraries acquire catalogs from each Station for selection, and develop their own indexing systems. The Monthly Checklist of State Publications indexes many of the Agricultural Experiment Station and Extension Service publications. Another index which includes these publications is the Bibliography of Agriculture.

8
Locating Literature Through Computer Retrieval

Introduction

"Database searching" is a term used for literature searching
through the use of a computer. Databases are generated by
businesses and organizations which often publish both the
abstracts or indexes and the corresponding machine readable
tapes (databases). An example of an organization which produces both is the Biosciences Information Services. They
publish <u>Biological Abstracts</u> and <u>Biological Abstracts/RRM</u>
(abstracts) and produce BIOSIS PREVIEWS (machine readable
tapes). The information in the abstracts and indexes, citations to journal articles and other types of literature, is
essentially the same or close to that in the machine readable
tapes.

These databases are sold to vendors. The vendors adapt their
retrieval service to libraries, research organizations, private businesses, and individuals. There are three major
vendors handling scientific material: DIALOG Information
Services, Inc., Systems Development Corporation, and Bibliographic Retrieval Service. (The information retrieval
systems of these vendors are called respectively, DIALOG,
ORBIT, and BRS. Each of these systems has its own command
language.) An organization which is also a vendor is the
National Library of Medicine, which both produces tapes for
and sells the service called MEDLINE.

Libraries, research organizations, private businesses, and
individuals, which are billed by the vendors for their services, may pass on all or part of the cost of searching to
the individual requesting the search. Libraries vary in
their charges to the user. College and university libraries
often have many librarians trained to perform searches for
their users. Also, a librarian can recommend whether a
search is best done on the computer or whether the printed
abstracts and indexes would do just as well.

In order to perform a search, the operator or librarian sits at a terminal which looks much like a typewriter. The terminal is connected to the database service (DIALOG Information Services, Inc., Systems Development Corporation, Bibliographic Retrieval Service, or the National Library of Medicine) by a telephone line. The queries are entered at the terminal and the message is transmitted to the computer. The response of the computer is typed out or displayed at the terminal. The end result is a printout of a bibliography, or if there are no citations on the subject then the computer indicates that also.

"Databases and Their Services" is a chart in Appendix III listing subject areas and the science databases which fall into those areas. The database services are the DIALOG, ORBIT, BRS, and National Library of Medicine computer systems.

Literature searching through the use of the computer is a valuable tool. It is time saving for the searcher, and although there are some disadvantages, the advantages usually outweigh them. The primary disadvantage is the cost. Advantages and disadvantages are listed below.

Advantages of Database Searching

1. A database search covers a great number of publications which can be searched at one time. One BIOSIS file (Biological Abstracts and Biological Abstracts/RRM or Bioresearch Index) may be searched from 1981 until the present. The file COMPREHENSIVE DISSERTATION INDEX (Dissertation Abstracts) from 1861 to the present is searchable through its database.

2. A database search saves a great deal of the researcher's time. Generally speaking, the librarian may interview the researcher for 10 to 30 minutes. The terminal time may be 5 to 20 minutes. The above times are usually much faster than a comparable search in a printed index or abstract.

3. There are more entry points in the database files than the printed indexes and abstracts. For example, journal titles can be searched in COMPENDEX and CA SEARCH, but not in the printed indexes and abstracts they cover. There are some files which do not have a comparable printed index. The CHEMNAME database is an example.

4. Several terms may be searched at the same time. For example, the terms "communication," "language" and "honey bee" may be searched all at once to give citations on honey bee dance language.

5. The keywords in the search are not limited to those words found in lists (controlled vocabulary), but may be words (free text searching) which, for example, occur in the titles or abstracts of articles.

6. The terms can be coordinated with "OR," "AND" or "NOT."
If it is an "OR" combination, then either term will be chosen.
Any citation dealing with "language" will be chosen and any
citation with "communication" will be chosen. If the statement is honey bee language, "AND" logic may be used to select
honey bee "AND" language. In the "AND" combination, the
citation must concern both honey bee and language. A "NOT"
statement may limit also. It may be desirable to exclude
books from the search; thus the statement would be honey bee
dance language "NOT" books.

7. It is possible to search two or more forms of the same
word at the same time. Truncation is a method of doing this.
"Apples" can be truncated to "apple?" in DIALOG to pick up
both "apple" and "apples" with one entry. In an ORBIT search
"apples" can be truncated with "apple#" or "apple:." BRS
will truncate "apples" to "apple$." The words "communicating,"
"communicate," "communication," or "communicative" can be
truncated to "communicat."

8. Words can be linked which appear together or separated
by other words. DIALOG links words as follows: Supernumerary
chromosomes will be supernumerary(w)chromosomes, honey bee
will be honey(w)bee. ORBIT links words with an "AND" to give
"honeyANDbee" or with a "(w)" to give "honey(w)bee," and BRS
links words with "ADJ" to give "honeyADJbee."

9. It is possible to match terms such as an author and a
subject, or a year and an author, or a subject with another
subject. For example, the author Carl von Frish could be
combined with honey bee to retrieve his research concerning
honey bees.

10. The search can be narrowed or broadened as needed. If
there are many citations, a search may be limited to articles
in English or to a given time period.

11. An update search can be done very easily. The last
month or current year can be easily searched on line.

12. Database searching allows the searcher to switch files
without resubmitting terms. A search may begin in BIOSIS
PREVIEWS (Biological Abstracts and Biological Abstracts/RRM
or Bioresearch Index) on the subject of the honey bee and
continue in a different file such as AGRICOLA (Bibliography
of Agriculture).

13. The most recent citations from a database may be more
recent than the printed index citations since the printed
indexes are produced from the computer tapes.

14. The printout at the terminal or offline print (which is
sent through the mail) is more convenient than copying the
citations from the printed index or abstracts.

15. Some databases which correspond to printed sources
include citations in the databases not available in the
printed source.

Disadvantages of Database Searching

1. Database searching is expensive since the vendor charges
for the services. The cost of a search may range from $5.00
to $20.00 or more. Cost varies with time spent on the com-
puter, number of citations printed, and the database.
AGRICOLA (database for agriculture) is less expensive than
many databases, while SCISEARCH (database for science) is
more expensive. The cost is about $20.00 to $165.00 per
hour for a typical database search. It should be noted that
since the manual searcher's time is valuable, database searching is an advantage.

2. Not all the citations retrieved are relevent since the
computer combines logically and not intellectually. An
example is "ribonucleotides" combined with "ribosomes;" this
combination gives several citations but the association of
the two terms as a search topic does not match intellectually.

3. Most databases are limited in how far back the literature
is covered. BIOSIS PREVIEWS (database for Biological
Abstracts and Biological Abstracts/RRM or Bioresearch Index)
encompasses the literature from 1969 to the present. Most
databases do not cover the literature much earlier than 1970.
One exception is COMPREHENSIVE DISSERTATION ABSTRACTS which
includes Ph.D. dissertations back to 1861.

4. All variations of words and their synonyms must be
entered at the computer terminal to retrieve the articles.
The computer does not do the thinking.

5. Usually words rather than concepts are the only input the
computer database accepts. BIOSIS PREVIEWS is an example of
a database which does use concepts. Some of its concept codes
are EVOLUTION, GENETICS AND CYTOGENETICS-ANIMAL, and REPRO-
DUCTIVE SYSTEM-ANATOMY.

6. Although database searching saves much time, there is a
waiting period before receiving the offline prints of the
citations. Offline prints are desirable because they are
less expensive. The waiting time is determined mostly by the
time required for the postal service.

Steps in Doing a Database Search

The following are some suggestions in preparing for a database search.

Preparation:

1. State the search topic in sentence form. This is necessary so the searcher can combine the search terms properly.

2. Narrow the search. Avoid being too general.

3. List all the appropriate key terms and synonyms.

4. Find additional terms in a dictionary or thesaurus.

5. Do a brief search in one or more indexes or abstracts
    a. for more terms,
    b. to narrow the topic if need be,
    c. to choose the best database for the search.

Execution:

Make arrangements with a librarian or company to do the search.

The database searcher uses logic to specify which information is retrieved from the computer. This logic is illustrated in the following section.

An Example of Computer Searching and Computer Logic

In order to illustrate computer logic, the following example for a search topic is used following the format of the DIALOG command language.

> "I want to retrieve citations on the fattening
> of calves."

After the search statement is formulated, the elements of the statement need to be identified. Then, the searcher must decide whether to use keywords or to use other terms, such as codes, to retrieve each element. If keywords are used, the searcher needs to identify possible synonyms. For this example, "calf" would be an additional word to add.

The computer uses Boolean logic to combine terms or sets, which may be two or more terms combined by an OR, AND, or NOT logic.

First the searcher asks the computer to select "calves."
The computer prints the following:

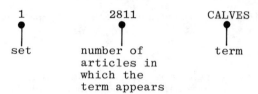

The searcher then selects "calf" and the computer prints the
following:

       2   1248   CALF

Next the searcher instructs the computer to combine two terms
with an "OR" since articles containing either or both terms
are wanted (see shaded area).

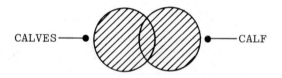

The computer printout is as follows:

Since all articles on "calves" or "calf" are not wanted, the
searcher instructs the computer to select "fattening." The
computer responds as follows:

       4   1660   FATTENING*

The searcher instructs the computer to combine "set 3" and
"set 4" with "AND" logic.

       5   124   3   AND   4

*In the actual search "fattening" was truncated to
 "fatten?"

In the "AND" combination only the articles about fattening of calves or calf will be retrieved. The shaded area in the diagram below indicates what the computer will retrieve.

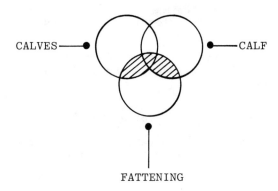

CALVES   CALF

FATTENING

Computer Searches Illustrating Logic

This section illustrates four computer searches from the major vendors. Included are terminal printouts with explanation of the printout elements.

The first three searches, DIALOG, ORBIT, and BRS, show how vendors differ in the way the operator and computer interact at the terminal. The same search for the same database has been carried out in all three cases. These searches illustrate the "AND" and "OR" logic, and the question is treated in this way to show this type of logic all three ways.

Another item to note about the first three searches is the way in which a keyword and another form of that keyword can be treated. The term used for this is truncation. In DIALOG, for example, fattening is truncated to "FATTEN?" to retrieve both fatten and fattening.

The fourth search, MEDLINE, illustrates another form of logic, the "AND NOT" logic. In this case the search statement is different from the other searches.

AN EXPLANATION OF THE TERMINAL PRINTOUT USING DIALOG

1   DIALOG uses a question mark to ask the user to respond. The user responds by entering "begin" and the file number of the database.

2   DIALOG uses a question mark to ask the user to respond. The user responds by selecting "calf" and "calves" and combining them with "or" logic.

3   DIALOG responds by indicating the presence of 1248 citations in which "CALF" occurs and 2811 citations in which "CALVES" occurs.

4   DIALOG displays the set number "1" and totals the number of citations (3993) containing "CALF" and "CALVES."

5   DIALOG uses a question mark to ask the user to respond. The user responds by selecting "fatten?." "Fattening" is truncated with "?"; so variations of "fatten" will be recorded.

6   DIALOG responds by indicating the presence of 1660 citations in set number "2" with the word "FATTEN?."

7   DIALOG uses a question mark to ask the user to respond. The user responds by combining sets "1" and "2" with "AND" logic.

8   DIALOG responds by indicating the presence of 124 citations when combining set numbers "1" and "2."

9   DIALOG uses a question mark to ask the user to respond. The user responds by asking DIALOG to print out offline the citations with term contained in set "3", in the form of format "5", and for citations "1" through "124."

10   Title of Article

11   Authors of article

12   Address of first author

13   Journal, volume, issue, year, pages, illustrations

14   Language

15   Number of references in article

16   A non-United States publication sponsored by the United States Department of Agriculture

17   Document type

18   Section heading

EXAMPLE OF A SEARCH USING DIALOG

Search statement: I want to retrieve citations on the
fattening of calves.

Terminal printout:

① ? begin 10

② ? select calf or calves

③ 1248 CALF

2811 CALVES

④ 1   3993   CALF OR CALVES

⑤ ? select fatten?

⑥ 2   1660 FATTEN?

⑦ ? combine 1 and 2

⑧ 3   124   1 AND 2

⑨ ? print 3/5/1-124

Example of offline printout:

⑩ A comparative study of the effects of feeding cereals
(corn, barley) to fattening Iraqui calves.
⑪ Al-Mallah, M.Y.; Mohammad, A.S. Dahal, I.A.M.
⑫ Mosul, Iraq, , College of Agriculture and Forestry,
Mosul University.
⑬ Mesopotamia journal of agriculture. v. 13 (2) , 1978.
p. 19-28.   ill.
⑭ Languages: ENGLISH ; ARABIC
⑮ 15 ref.
⑯ Subfile: OTHER USDA;
⑰ Document Type: ARTICLE
⑱ Section Headings: ANIMAL NUTRITION(L500)

AN EXPLANATION OF THE TERMINAL PRINTOUT USING ORBIT

1   User tells ORBIT which database to use.

2   ORBIT uses this phrase to ask user to respond.

3   The user responds by selecting "CALF" and "CALVES" and combining them with "OR" logic.

4   ORBIT responds by indicating the presence of 2849 citations in which "CALF" occurs and 6102 citations in which "CALVES" occurs.

5   ORBIT displays set "1" and totals the number of citations (8843) containing "CALF" and "CALVES."

6   ORBIT uses this phrase to tell the user to respond.

7   The user responds by selecting "FATTEN:."

8   ORBIT responds by indicating the presence of 4550 citations in set number "2" with the word "FATTEN:."

9   ORBIT uses this phrase to ask the user to respond.

10 The user responds by combining sets "1" and "2" with "AND" logic.

11 ORBIT responds by indicating that set "3" has 445 citations by combining set "1" and "2."

12 ORBIT uses this phrase to ask the user to respond.

13 The user responds by asking ORBIT to print the citations.

EXAMPLE OF A SEARCH USING ORBIT

Search statement: I want to retrieve citations on the
fattening of calves.

Terminal printout:

① FILE AGRICOLA

② SS 1 /C?
   USER:
③ CALF OR CALVES

④ PROG:
          OCCURS TERM
             2849 CALF
             6102 CALVES
⑤ SS 1 PSTG (8843)

⑥ SS 2 /C?
   USER:
⑦ ALL FATTEN:

⑧ PROG:
   SS 2 PSTG (4450)

⑨ SS 3/ C?
   USER:
⑩ 1 AND 2

⑪ PROG:
          OCCURS TERM
   SS 3 PSTG (445)

⑫ SS 4 /C?
   USER:
⑬ PRTOFF

Example of offline printout:

ACCESSION NUMBER	769094569
TITLE	A NOTE ON THE VALUE OF DRIED CITRUS PULP AND GRAPE MARC AS BARLEY REPLACE-MENTS IN CALF FATTENING DIETS
AUTHORS	HADJIPANAYIOTOU, M
AUTHORS	LOUCA, A
SOURCE	ANIM PROD, 23 (1): 129-132.
PUBLICATION DATE	1976 AUG
DOCUMENT TYPE	ARTICLE
LANGUAGE	ENG
NAL CAL NUMBER	49 AN55
PRIMARY CATEGORY CODE	251500

NOTE: This file is no longer available on ORBIT.

Note: SDC has withdrawn this file but the strategy is representative
      for all the SDC database files.

AN EXPLANATION OF THE TERMINAL PRINTOUT USING BRS

1 BRS tells the user to respond. The user responds by typing in the database name, "cain."

2 BRS responds by telling the user that he/she is connected with the database, "cain."

3 BRS tells the user to respond.

4 BRS displays set number "1" which tells the user to respond. The user directs BRS to select "calf" and "calves" and combine them with "OR" logic.

5 BRS indicates that there are 12176 citations in which "calf" or "calves" occur.

6 BRS displays set number "2" which tells the user to respond. The user responds by asking BRS how many citations contain the word "fatten$."

7 BRS indicates that there are 5930 citations in which "fatten$" occurs.

8 BRS displays set number "3" which tells the user to respond. The user responds by combining sets "1" and "2" with "AND" logic.

9 BRS tells the user that there are 544 citations combining set numbers "1" and "2."

10 BRS displays set number "4" which tells the user to respond. The user responds by asking BRS to print off line "all" citations in set "3," using the full record format, and put "J. Smith, agriculture library" on the title page of the printout.

11 BRS tells the user that the above request has been done.

12 Accession number

13 Authors

14 Title of article

15 Source

16 National Agricultural Library call number

17 Year

18 Language

19 Note

20 Publication type

21 National Agricultural Library category code

EXAMPLE OF A SEARCH USING BRS

Search statement: I want to retrieve citations on the fattening of calves.

Terminal printout:

①ENTER DATA BASE NAME_: cain

②BRS/CAIN/1970 - OCT 1982

③BRS - SEARCH MODE - ENTER QUERY

    ④1_: calf or calves
    ⑤RĒSULT 12176

    ⑥2_: fatten$
    ⑦RĒSULT 5930

    ⑧3_: 1 and 2
    ⑨RĒSULT 544

    ⑩4_: ..po 3 all/doc=all/id-j. smith; agriculture
       library
⑪YOUR OFFLINE QUERY HAS BEEN SAVED UNDER THE NAME OF Qu143

Example of offline printout:

⑫AN 79088724
⑬AU EL-HUSSEINY, O. ABOU-MANDOUR, M.
⑭TI NUTRITIONAL AND ECONOMICAL STUDIES ON FATTENING BEEF
    CALVES USING DRY RATION DURING SUMMER AND WINTER
    SEASONS.
⑮SO ANN AGRIC SCI (MOSHTOHOR). MOSHTOHOR, ZAGAZIG UNIV.
    FACULTY OF AGRICULTURAL SCIENCE. 1978. V. 9.
    P. 215-222. ILL.
⑯CN S341.A5..
⑰YR 78..
⑱LG EN..
⑲NT 8 REF.
⑳PT A.
㉑CC 2515.

AN EXPLANATION OF THE TERMINAL PRINTOUT USING MEDLINE

1   The National Library of Medicine system tells the user
    he/she is in the MEDLINE file.

2   MEDLINE tells the user to respond.

3   The user responds by typing in the keyword "caffeine"
    and limiting it to adverse effects.

4   MEDLINE responds by telling the user in set "1" there
    are "57" articles in which the subject adverse effects
    of caffeine occurs.

5   MEDLINE tells the user to respond.

6   MEDLINE combines set "1" with "and not" foreign; thus
    only the articles in English on adverse effects of
    caffeine will be retrieved.

7   MEDLINE asks the user if he/she wishes to search for an
    additional amount of time to complete the search request.

8   The user responds by saying yes ("y").

9   MEDLINE responds by telling the user in set "2" there
    are 51 articles in English in which the subject adverse
    effects of caffeine occurs.

10 MEDLINE tells the user to respond.

11 The user responds by typing in print "1" citation.

12 Author

13 Title

14 Source journal, date, volume, issue, pages

EXAMPLE OF A SEARCH USING MEDLINE

Search statement: I want to retrieve citations in English
on the adverse effects of caffeine.

Terminal printout:

(1) HELLO FROM ELHILL AT SUNY
YOU ARE NOW CONNECTED TO THE MEDLINE FILE.

(2) SS 1 /C?
USER:
(3) caffeine/ae
(4) PROG:
SS (1) PSTG (57)

(5) SS 2 /C?
USER:
(6) 1 and not for
(7) PROG:
TIME OVFLOW: CONT? (Y/N)

(8) USER:
y
(9) PROG:
SS (2) PSTG (51)

(10) SS 3 /C?
USER:
(11) prt 1
PROG:

Example of offline printout:

(12) AU — Holloway WR Jr
(13) TI — Caffeine: effects of acute and chronic exposure
on the behavior of neonatal rats.
(14) SO — Neurobehav Toxicol Teratol 1982 Jan-Feb;
4(1):21-32

U.S. Government database
National Library of Medicine

COMPUTER SEARCH USING DIALOG
WITH THE DATABASE SCISEARCH

SCISEARCH (database for <u>Science Citation Index</u> and <u>Current</u>
<u>Contents</u>) adds another dimension to database searching. The
example given below illustrates a computer terminal printout
which corresponds to the citations found in the Citation
Index and the Source Index of <u>Science Citation Index</u>. The
Citation Index allows one to use an earlier paper such as
the one listed below by Watson and Crick, and find later
papers relating to Watson and Crick's work. (See the section
entitled "Science Citation Index--Citation Approach" in
Chapter 5 for a more detailed explanation.)

AN EXPLANATION OF THE TERMINAL PRINTOUT USING
DIALOG WITH THE DATABASE SCISEARCH

1   DIALOG uses a question mark to ask the user to respond.
    The user responds by entering "begin" and the file
    number of the database.

2   DIALOG uses a question mark to ask the user to respond.
    The user asks DIALOG to expand the cit<u>ed</u> reference
    "Watson, J.D."

3   DIALOG expands the cit<u>ed</u> reference "Watson, J.D." The
    expand command lists those names and references just
    before and after "Watson, J.D."

4   DIALOG uses a question mark to ask the user to respond.
    The user responds by selecting "e5."

5   DIALOG displays set "1" and says there are 45 references
    in which J.D. Watson's 1953 paper appearing in the
    journal, <u>Nature</u>, volume 171, page 737 was quoted.

6   DIALOG uses a question mark to ask the user to respond.
    The user asks DIALOG to type set "1," format "3,"
    reference "1."

7   Set "1," format "3," reference "1."

8   DIALOG accession number, OATS order number to order the
    article from the Institute for Scientific Information,
    14 references in the cit<u>ing</u> author's article.

9   Title of cit<u>ing</u> authors' article.

10 Names of cit<u>ing</u> authors.

11 Cit<u>ing</u> authors' journal, volume, issue, pages, year.

EXAMPLE OF A SEARCH USING DIALOG WITH THE DATABASE SCISEARCH

Search statement: I want to retrieve articles on DNA
relating to J. D. Watson and F. H. C. Crick's 1953 article
on the structure of DNA.

The paper referred to is the following:

Watson, J. D. and F. H. C. Crick. "Molecular Structure of
    Nucleic Acids. A Structure for Deoxyribose Nucleic
    Acids." Nature 171:737-38, 1953.

Terminal printout:

① ? begin 34
② ? expand cr=watson jd
③ Ref   Items   Index-term
    E1   1   CR=WATSON JBG, 1979,
                    V54, P77
    E2   1   CR=WATSON JC, 1980,
                    V87, P184
    E3   *CR=WATSON JD
    E4   1   CR=WATSON JD, 1953,
                    V171, P263
    E5   45   CR=WATSON JD, 1953,
                    V171, P737
    E6   1   CR=WATSON JD, 1953,
                    V171, P740
                                        -more-
④ ? select e5
                ⑤ 1   45 CR=WATSON JD, 1953, V171, P737
⑥ ? type 1/3/1
⑦ 1/3/1
⑧ 0842703 OATS ORDER#: NP613   14 REFS
⑨   THE STRUCTURE OF DNA   (ENGLISH)
⑩   VARUGHESE KI; REDHEENDRAN R
⑪   SPECULATIONS IN SCIENCE AND TECHNOLOGY, V5, N1,
    P49-50, 1982

9
Finding Specialized Reference Sources

Introduction

Reference books are books to be consulted for factual information rather than read from cover to cover. Listed below are
the major functions of types of reference books. This chapter
does not attempt to cover the many reference books available
in the fields of science, technology, and agriculture.
Instead it lists some of the guides to the literature which
include most of the reference books in these fields.

Types of Reference Books

Roughly speaking, reference sources may be divided into two
main classes:

(A)   Compendiums of one form or another, which furnish
information and
(B)   Bibliographic aids which indicate where the
information may be found.

A.   Reference sources in type A, which supply information on
general and special subjects, may be divided into the
following types:

> 1.   <u>Dictionaries</u> give definitions, derivations, usages,
> and proper spelling of words. Example: <u>McGraw-Hill</u>
> <u>Dictionary of Scientific & Technical Terms</u>, McGraw-Hill,
> 1978.

> 2.   <u>Encyclopedias</u> include articles which are usually
> concise.   The encyclopedias' topics may include all
> subjects or they may be limited to a given field.   The
> articles define and describe subjects.   They may be
> signed, initialed, or unsigned.   They often contain
> bibliographic references. Example: <u>McGraw-Hill</u>
> <u>Encyclopedia of Science & Technology</u>, McGraw-Hill, 1977.

3. <u>Yearbooks</u> have two functions: to update a larger work, often an encyclopedia, and to give the year's more important events or discoveries. Example: <u>McGraw-Hill Yearbook of Science and Technology</u>, McGraw-Hill, 1983.

4. <u>Biographical Dictionaries</u> contain biographical sketches giving information about the lives of individuals. Often the sketches are concise. Example: <u>American Men & Women of Science</u>, Bowker, 1982.

5. <u>Directories</u> list names and addresses of persons, organizations, and institutions. Example: <u>American Medical Directory</u>, American Medical Association, 1982.

6. <u>Handbooks and Manuals</u> may contain tables, formulas, graphs, diagrams, specifications, and definitions. The information is brief usually and is often useful in solving problems. Example: <u>Bergey's Manual of Determinative Bacteriology</u>, Williams & Wilkins, 1974.

7. <u>Atlases</u> contain collections of maps (they may have material explaining them) illustrating such things as plant distribution, animal distribution, soil types, climate, crop distribution, or livestock distribution. Example: <u>World Atlas of Agriculture</u>, International Association of Agricultural Economists, 1969--. <u>Atlas of Human Anatomy</u>, Saunders, 1971.

8. <u>Gazetteers</u> are dictionaries listing place names with brief descriptions. These descriptions may include population, location, economic importance, and historical facts. Example: <u>The Columbia-Lippincott Gazetter of the World</u>, Columbia University Press, 1962.

B. Reference sources in type B, which are bibliographic aids, may be divided into the following types:

1. <u>Indexes</u> make journal articles, reviews, dissertations, reports, government documents and proceedings accessible, usually by subject, in such a way that the user will not find it necessary to look through each individual journal for articles. An index includes a citation only. Example: <u>Bibliography of Agriculture</u>.

2. <u>Abstracts</u> function the same as indexes (see number 1), but they have in addition an abstract or summary of the article in question. Example: <u>Biological Abstracts</u>.

3. <u>Guides to the Literature</u> cover literature of different disciplines and often give lists of reference books with or without annotations. Example: H. R. Malinowsky and J. M. Richardson, <u>Science and Engineering Literature: A Guide to Reference Sources</u>, Libraries Unlimited, 1980.

4. Bibliographies are extensive lists of books, journal
articles, or other publications which are arranged in
some logical order. Bibliographies often deal with a
specific topic. They may have annotations which are
referred to as "annotated bibliographies." Example:
Index to American Botanical Literature, 1886-1966,
G. K. Hall, 1969. A Bibliography of Eastern Asiatic
Botany, Arnold Arboretum of Harvard University, 1938.

5. Catalogs of Library Collections contain lists of
publications of a library's collection or holdings.
They are usually arranged by author and/or subject
alphabetically. Example: National Union Catalog,
Library of Congress, 1979--. Dictionary Catalog of the
National Agricultural Library, 1862-1965, Rowman and
Littlefield, 1967-70.

How to Find Reference Books

Reference books are too numerous to list in this guide;
therefore the authors have chosen to list a few "guides to
the literature," which list and/or discuss reference books.
A brief description accompanies each guide. In order to
find the most recently published guide one should consult
the card catalog either for the latest edition by a known
author or by a subject heading leading to guides to the
literature. The authors have chosen to include here guides
which list reference books recommended for a library collection rather than guides which include books which are not
reference books. An example of a guide of the latter type
is Books for College Libraries, American Library Association,
1975.

Guides to the Literature

General Science

Grogan, D. Science and Technology; An Introduction to the
    Literature. 4th ed. London: Clive Bingley, 1982.

Grogan's book is a description of different types of literature such as encyclopedias, handbooks, books "in the field,"
periodicals, and indexing and abstracting services. The book
has a narrative style which mentions specific sources only as
examples, and the author does not seem to be seeking an
exhaustive coverage of sources. Unlike many guides, the
text is not a bibliography or an annotated bibliography.
The book's examples of sources given in the discussion are
representative of many countries. American and British
sources are mentioned the most. There is a subject index,
but no author or title index.

Chen, C., ed. Scientific and Technical Information Sources.
    Cambridge, Mass.: MIT Press, 1977.

Chen has an extensive list of scientific, technical, and
agricultural sources. The guide is divided into chapters
dealing with sources such as dictionaries, encyclopedias,
and handbooks. Each chapter is divided further into disciplines, for example, physics, biological sciences, and
various fields of engineering. The sources listed have
brief annotations. There is some explanatory material in
addition to the annotations. Databases are listed in a
chart with their vendors. Although many databases have been
added since the publishing of Chen's book, the major disciplines are represented. The table of contents is extensive,
and an author index is included.

Lasworth, E. J. Reference Sources in Science and Technology.
    Metuchen, N.J.: Scarecrow Press, 1972.

Lasworth's guide is arranged by type of reference book or
source and then subdivided by discipline. For example,
"Handbooks" would be a type of reference book and "Biological
Sciences" would be a subdivision. Much of the guide is an
unannotated bibliography, but included are discussions of
such items as search strategy and how to use the card catalog.
There is also an explanation of each type of reference book
or source throughout the guide. The guide contains two
indexes--an author index and a title index.

Malinowsky, H. R. and J. M. Richardson. Science and
    Engineering Literature; A Guide to Reference Sources.
    3d ed. Littleton, Colo.: Libraries Unlimited, 1980.

Malinowsky divides his guide into subject fields or disciplines and discusses each type of reference source or tool
that pertains to the discipline. For example, "Biomedical
Sciences" as a discipline and "Handbooks and Laboratory
Guides" as a reference source are used. Each source is
annotated. A short section on bibliographic databases is
included. The subject sections are introduced by a description of the discipline represented in that section. The
guide is well indexed with its "author-title-subject index."

Agriculture

Blanchard, J. R. and L. Farrell, eds. Guide to Sources
    for Agricultural and Biological Research. Berkeley:
    University of California Press, 1981.

This long awaited publication gives world wide coverage of
agricultural literature and includes all areas of the discipline. Such subjects in agriculture and biology as plant
science, crop production, crop protection, animal sciences,
physical sciences, food and nutrition, environmental sciences,

and social sciences are covered. The introduction includes
a section on search strategy and networks. The sources are
evaluated and described. Databases, when available, are
mentioned. The author, subject and title indexes provide
good access.

Biology

Bottle, R. T., and H. V. Wyatt, eds. The Use of Biological
    Literature. 2d ed. Hamden, Conn.: Archon Books, 1971.

One chapter covers "Libraries and Their Use," several
chapters present the types of literature, several chapters
discuss specific fields and their literature. The guide
itself is written in narrative style. There is much background explanation of the materials' importance to biologists.

Davis, E. B. Using the Biological Literature: A Practical
    Guide. New York: Dekker, 1981.

The introductory chapter reviews the history of biology and
its literature. Most of the remaining chapters each deal
with a biological discipline and list reference books.
Almost all are annotated.

Smith, R. C., W. M. Reid, and A. E. Luchsinger. Smith's
    Guide to the Literature of Life Sciences. 9th ed.
    Minneapolis, Minn.: Burgess Pub. Co., 1980.

This guide is a "how to" source. The aim of the guide is to
introduce the most useful sources in the library to the
biologist, and to help the biologist report to the scientific
community. The first chapter is entitled "The Scientist and
Research Libraries" and covers a variety of topics. Other
chapters cover the library arrangement and card catalog,
library sources and searching techniques needed to write a
paper, and the preparation of a paper. Bibliographic databases are also discussed. Library assignments are included
at the end of each chapter.

Chemistry

Bottle, R. T., ed. Use of Chemical Literature. 3d ed.
    London: Butterworths, 1979.

Since R. T. Bottle, the editor, is from Britain, the book has
a definite British emphasis. The guide is written from a
chemist's standpoint and has much more explanative text than
many guides. Explanation of items is on a specialized level.
The guide has a chapter on "Libraries and Their Use,"
several chapters covering types of literature, and several
chapters on specific fields or aspects of chemistry.

Mellon, M. G. Chemical Publications; Their Nature and Use.
    4th ed. New York: McGraw-Hill, 1965.

This work contains extensive background material which helps
the reader become familiar with chemical literature and understand its usefulness to the discipline. Mellon discusses
periodicals, government documents, patents, monographs, text-
books, abstracts and indexes, reference books, and searches.
Also included is an extensive section of library exercises.

Antony, A. Guide to Basic Information Sources in Chemistry.
    New York: J. Norton, 1979.

The chapter organization of the guide departs from the usual
pattern of science guides, which is refreshing. As an
example, a full chapter is devoted to Chemical Abstracts, and
another to bibliographic searching by computer. The handbooks
of Beilstein and Gmelin share a chapter. The final chapter
outlines search strategy through the use of case studies.
Each chapter has an introduction which is usually followed by
a list of sources. Of the many sources included, most have
annotations.

Computer Science

Myers, D. Computer Science Resources: A Guide to
    Professional Literature. White Plains, N.Y.:
    Knowledge Industry Publications, 1981.

This guide is a compilation of several thousand reference
sources which includes journals, indexes, abstracts,
directories, dictionaries, handbooks, newsletters, conference publications, software resources, and programming
language sources. Current books are also covered. Each
section of this guide consists of a brief introduction
followed by a listing of sources. The table of contents
outlines the chapters. No additional indexing is provided.

Pritchard, A. A Guide to Computer Literature; An Introductory
    Survey of the Sources of Information. 2d ed. Hamden,
    Conn.: Linnet Books, 1972.

The first half of the book is devoted primarily to types of
literature which are primary sources in computer science.
Those types discussed are periodicals, reports, government
publications, trade literature, theses, patents, conferences,
and translations. The above chapters also include reference
materials in relation to specific literature types. The
latter part of the guide deals with reference publications
and other secondary sources such as abstracts, indexes, handbooks, annual reviews, bibliographies, dictionaries, and
standards.

Engineering

Mildren, K. W., ed. <u>Use of Engineering Literature</u>. London:
     Butterworths, 1976.

This British publication (which includes American literature
also) is extensive and consists of over 620 pages. Both
professionals in the field of engineering and librarians have
contributed chapters edited by Mildren. Many more than the
standard reference tools are included. There are discussions
of journals, conferences, theses, translations, reports,
patents, and standards. One chapter is devoted to literature
searching. The last two-thirds of the book are devoted to
disciplines within the field of engineering.

Mount, E. <u>Guide to Basic Information Sources in Engineering</u>.
     New York: J. Norton, 1976.

This guide is written for engineering students and researcher
It is selective and includes a section concerning how to use
libraries. The sections have introductions and lists of
reference books which are annotated. Discussions of the type
of literature such as periodicals, reports, symposia, specifications, standards, catalogs, tables, and statistics make
up a good portion of the guide. There is a useful index
including authors, titles and subjects in the main body of
the book. The simplicity of this guide makes it usable by a
less sophisticated audience than many other guides and it
can be recommended to the beginning student.

Parsons, S. A. J. <u>How to Find Out About Engineering</u>. Oxford
     Pergamon Press, 1972.

This guide discusses numerous divisions of engineering. The
fields include mechanical, electrical, civil, chemical,
nuclear, production, and agricultural engineering. The book
has sections on careers, finding information, libraries, and
reference materials. Like many British guides, this publication is organized to emphasize the disciplines covered
rather than to list items in a bibliography. The index may
be used to find specific reference books and information
relating to them.

Geology

Ward, D. C. and M. W. Wheeler. <u>Geologic Reference Sources</u>;
     <u>A Subject and Regional Bibliography of Publications and</u>
     <u>Maps in the Geologic Sciences</u>. 2d ed. Metuchen, N.J.:
     Scarecrow Press, 1981.

This guide covers the literature of the world with some
emphasis on English language publications. The guide lists
sources much like a bibliography. Some sources are annotated

The book is divided into three sections. The "General
Section" covers history, current awareness, indexes,
abstracts, and more. The "Subject Section" lists by subject
reference books, texts, treatises, and other specialized
literature. The "Regional Section" divides the world into
regions and includes reference works, texts, treatises, maps
and other specialized material.

Wood, D. N., ed. Use of Earth Science Literature. Hamden,
    Conn.: Archon Books, 1973.

The editor states that the aim of the guide is "to present a
general picture of the structure of the literature and to
illustrate it with examples." Several chapters are devoted
to defining the types of literature such as reviews, periodical articles, proceedings, maps, and reference books.
Methods of literature searching are also described. The
latter two-thirds of the book discuss the various disciplines
of the earth sciences.

Mathematics

Pemberton, J. E. How to Find Out in Mathematics; A Guide to
    Sources of Information. 2d ed. Elmsford, N.Y.:
    Pergamon Press, 1969.

This small guide is written in narrative style, and the
author states that the book may be read in its entirety.
The book is also designed to be of reference value. Chapter
one discusses careers for mathematicians, chapter two discusses the organization of mathematical information and
libraries, and the remaining chapters discuss reference books
or mathematical topics with mention of reference books. The
index contains subjects, titles, and authors.

Medicine

Morton, L. T., ed. Use of Medical Literature. 2d ed.
    London: Butterworths, 1977.

The Use of Medical Literature is a British publication with,
for the most part, a different author for each chapter.
Morton writes the first chapter on "Libraries and Their Use."
The next chapters concern different types of literature,
followed by a chapter on databases. Most of the chapters
cover, in narrative form, different medical specializations
with discussions of the specialized types of literature.
Historical and biographical sources are covered in one of
the latter chapters. The final chapter explains how to
organize personal index files.

Roper, F. W. and J. A. Boorkman. <u>Introduction to Reference</u>
    <u>Sources in the Health Sciences</u>. Chicago: Medical
    Library Association, 1980.

The apparent intended audience of this book is the librarian
and library school student, but others can gain insight into
medical literature through careful reading also. Part I
explains organization of a reference collection. Parts II
and III discuss reference sources, both bibliographic and
informational. These latter two parts compose the major
portion of the book. The guide contains a good coverage of
bibliographic databases and especially the databases produced
by the National Library of Medicine. The book is primarily
text with sources listed at intervals.

Physics

Coblans, H., ed. <u>Use of Physics Literature</u>. London:
    Butterworths, 1975.

Although this publication is British it does not limit its
discussions to primarily British literature. It is equally
strong in American sources. The text is written in a narrative style with a brief introduction to each specialty and
discussions of the sources. There are many contributors to
the text. The first three chapters respectively are devoted
to an introduction, characteristics of physics literature,
and scientific libraries. Most of the remaining chapters
discuss specialized areas within the field of physics such
as astrophysics, crystallography, and theoretical physics.

Whitford, R. H. <u>Physics Literature; A Reference Manual</u>.
    2d ed. Metuchen, N. J.: Scarecrow Press, 1968.

This guide is written for college students. It does not
attempt to be an exhaustive list of reference sources. The
author presents his selection criteria on the first page of
the text. The guide is organized by approaches such as historical, biographical, experimental, as well as the bibliographical approach. Each approach discusses the reference
sources which are useful for the specific approach covered.

Yates, B. <u>How to Find Out About Physics; A Guide to Sources</u>
    <u>of Information Arranged by Decimal Classification.</u>
    Oxford: Pergamon Press, 1965.

Yates' guide is intended for a broad audience which includes
students, physicists, librarians, and the general public.
The book includes both discussions of information sources and
lists of materials.   The author includes Dewey classification
numbers with the sources.   Areas discussed are careers in
physics, reference books, documents, periodicals, abstracts,
societies, research organizations, and information centers.
Questions are at the end of each chapter.

10
Citing the Literature in a Bibliography

Introduction

The importance of using a style manual, which gives the form or style for citations in a bibliography, may not be apparent at first glance. Compare the styles below with the help of the chart on the next page. There are a variety of ways to cite journal articles; thus a style manual is essential in compilation of a bibliography.

It should be pointed out that the one major difference in the form of a citation for the sciences and the social sciences and humanities is that the science publications usually place the date of an article after the author rather than near the end of the citation.

Examples of Citations Using Different Style Manuals

Turabian, 1976, pages 33 and 36-37

> Paliwal, Y. C., and Tremaine, J. H. "Multiplication, Purification, and Properties of Ryegrass Mosaic Virus." Phytopathology 66 (April 1976):406-14.

Campbell, 1982, page 119 (journals, basic form, MLA)

> Paliwal, Y. C., and J. H. Tremaine. "Multiplication, Purification, and Properties of Ryegrass Mosaic Virus." Phytopathology, 66 (1976), 406-14.

Phytopathology (Journal)

> 1. Paliwal, Y. C., and Tremaine, J. H. 1976. Multiplication, purification, and properties of ryegrass mosaic virus. Phytopathology 55: 406-414.

Council of Biology Editors Style Manual, 1978, page 52

> 1. Paliwal, Y. C.; Tremaine, J. H. Multiplication, purification, and properties of ryegrass mosaic virus. Phytopathology 66:406-414; 1976.

COMPARISON OF STYLES
FOR
LITERATURE CITED IN BIBLIOGRAPHY

	TURABIAN	CAMPBELL	PHYTO-PATHOLOGY	COUNCIL OF BIOL. EDITORS
AUTHOR:				
a. Punctuation after first name	comma	comma	comma	semicolon
b. initials placement-second name	inverted	proper order	inverted	inverted
DATE:				
a. what is included?	month and year in parenthesis	year in parentheses comma after year	year only period following	year only period following
b. position in citation	near end of citation (after volume)	near end of citation	after author	at end of citation
TITLE OF ARTICLE:				
a. beginning letter capitalized each word of title	yes	yes	no	no
b. enclosed in quotation marks	yes	yes	no	no
c. followed by period	yes	yes	yes	yes
JOURNAL TITLE:				
a. underlined?	yes	yes	no	no
b. followed by comma?	no	yes	no	no
VOLUME:				
a. arabic numerals	yes	yes	yes	yes
PAGE:				
a. all digits used in inclusive pages	no	no	yes	yes

<u>List of Style Manuals</u>

Each journal determines a style for citations in the bibliography of an article. Sometimes the journal gives directions
for the form of its citations. A style manual may be useful
as a supplement to the journal form. The following is a list
of style manuals:

<u>General</u>

  Campbell, William G., Stephen V. Ballou, and Carole
   Slade. <u>Form and Style: Theses, Reports, Term</u>
   <u>Papers.</u> 6th ed. Boston: Houghton Mifflin Co.,
   1982.

  Dugdale, Kathleen. <u>A Manual of Form for Theses and</u>
   <u>Term Reports.</u> 5th ed. Bloomington, Ind.:
   Indiana University Bookstore, 1972.

  Turabian, Kate L. <u>Student's Guide for Writing</u>
   <u>College Papers.</u> 3d ed. Chicago: University
   of Chicago Press, 1976.

  U.S. Government Printing Office. <u>Style Manual.</u>
   Rev. ed. Washington: U.S. Govt. Print. Off.,
   1973.

<u>Biological Sciences</u>

  Council of Biology Editors. Committee on Form
   and Style. <u>Council of Biology Editors</u>
   <u>Style Manual: a Guide for Authors, Editors,</u>
   <u>and Publishers in the Biological Sciences.</u>
   4th ed. Arlington, Va.: American Institute
   of Biological Sciences, 1978.

<u>Chemistry</u>

  American Chemical Society. <u>Handbook for Authors</u>
   <u>of Papers in American Chemical Society</u>
   <u>Publications.</u> Washington: American Chemical
   Society, 1978.

<u>Engineering</u>

  Laird, Eleanor S. <u>Engineering Secretary's Complete</u>
   <u>Handbook.</u> 2d ed. Englewood Cliffs, N.J.:
   Prentice-Hall, 1967.

Mathematics

American Mathematical Society. Manual for Authors
of Mathematical Papers. Providence, R.I.:
American Mathematical Society, 1979.

Medicine

American Medical Association. Stylebook-Editorial
Manual. Littleton, Colo.: PSG Publishing Co.,
1976.

Physics

American Institute of Physics. Publication Board.
Style Manual for Guidance in the Preparation
of Papers for Journals. Rev. ed. New York:
The Institute, 1978.

Citing Government Documents

Because the subject oriented style manuals for scientific
topics tend to have little information on citing government
documents, a few examples of bibliography forms are given
here according to the authors' interpretation of Campbell.
When it is necessary to cite a government document, a form
taken from a general style manual (compatible with the
chosen scientific style) is recommended.

Statutes and Regulations

U.S. Const. art. II, § § 2-3.

This citation refers to the United States
Constitution, sections two and three of
article II.

16 U.S.C. § 668 (a) (1980 Supp. IV).

A statute is cited in the United States
Code, Title 16, Section 668 a, from the
1980 supplement volume IV.

10 C.F.R. § 2.104.

A regulation is cited from the Code of
Federal Regulations, Title 10, Section 2.104.

Court Cases

Legal citations appear as footnotes or in the body of the text. For bibliographies, the same form may be used.

>   Gottesman v. General Motors Corp.,
>   441 U.S. 932 (1978).
>
>   This citation is to a U.S. Supreme Court
>   decision contained in volume 441 of the
>   official reports of decisions of the
>   Supreme Court (United States Reports).

Congressional Publications

>   U.S. Cong. Senate. Committee on Foreign Relations.
>   Subcommittee on International Economic Policy.
>   The U.S. Stake in the Global Economy. Hearing,
>   97th Cong., 1st sess., 29 Feb. 1982. Washington,
>   D.C.: GPO, 1982.
>
>   Cong. Rec. 5 Mar. 1981, pp. 908-10.

Departmental Publications

>   U.S. Department of Education. Admission and Retention
>   Problems of Black Students at Seven Predominantly
>   White Universities. Washington, D.C.: GPO, 1982.

Appendix I
Abstracts and Indexes

Agriculture

Abstracts on Tropical Agriculture
Agrindex
Animal Breeding Abstracts +
Apicultural Abstracts +
Bibliography of Agriculture
Dairy Science Abstracts +
Fertilizer Abstracts
Field Crop Abstracts +
Forestry Abstracts +
Herbage Abstracts +
Horticultural Abstracts +
Nutrition Abstracts and Reviews. Series B. Livestock Feeds
    and Feeding +
Plant Breeding Abstracts +
Review of Applied Entomology. Series A. Agricultural +
Review of Applied Entomology. Series B. Medical and
    Veterinary +
Soils and Fertilizers +
The Veterinary Bulletin +
Weed Abstracts +
World Agricultural Economics and Rural Sociology Abstracts +

+ Commonwealth Agricultural Bureaux

Biology

Aerospace Medicine and Biology
Anatomy, Anthropology, Embryology and Histology *
Biological Abstracts
Biological Abstracts/RRM
Cambridge Scientific Abstracts (19 titles)
Clinical Biochemistry *
Developmental Biology and Teratology *
Ecological Abstracts
Endocrinology *
Excerpta Botanica
Genetics Abstracts
Helminthological Abstracts. Animal and Human Helminthology
Helminthological Abstracts. Plant Nematology
Human Genetics *
Immunology, Serology and Transplantation *
International Abstracts of Biological Sciences
Microbiology: Bacteriology, Mycology and Parasitology *
Oceanic Abstracts with Indexes
Physiology *
Review of Plant Pathology +
Virology *
Zoological Record

Chemistry

Analytical Abstracts
Biochemistry Abstracts (3 parts, Cambridge Scientific
    Abstracts)
Chemical Abstracts
Chemical Titles
Current Abstracts of Chemistry and Index Chemicus
Electroanalytical Abstracts
Gas and Liquid Chromatography Abstracts
Gas Chromatography Literature

+ Commonwealth Agricultural Bureaux
* Excerpta Medica abstracting service

Computer Science and Mathematics

Computer Abstracts
Computer and Information Systems Abstracts
Data Processing Digest
Mathematical Reviews
Science Abstracts. Series C. Computer and Control Abstracts

Engineering

Applied Mechanics Reviews
Ceramic Abstracts
Corrosion Abstracts
Electronics & Communication Abstracts
Energy Information Abstracts
Energy Index
Energy Review
Environment Abstracts
Environment Index
Graphics Arts Literature Abstracts
HRIS Abstracts
Lead Abstracts
Metals Abstracts
Operations Research/Management Science
Pollution Abstracts
Quality Control and Applied Statistics
Safety Science Abstracts (Cambridge Scientific Abstracts)
Science Abstracts. Series B. Electrical and Electronics
      Abstracts
Solid-Liquid Flow Abstracts
Solid State Abstracts Journal

Medicine

Aerospace Medicine and Biology
Excerpta Medica (51 titles)

Nutrition Abstracts and Reviews.   Series A.   Human and
        Experimental +
Index Medicus

Physics

Acoustics Abstracts
Bibliography and Index to Geology
INIS Atomindex
Science Abstracts.   Series A.   Physics Abstracts

Science and Technology

Food Science and Technology Abstracts
ISMEC (Cambridge Scientific Abstracts)
Science Research Abstracts (Cambridge Scientific Abstracts)
Textile Technology Digest
World Textile Abstracts

+ Commonwealth Agricultural Bureaux

Appendix II
Journals

Astronomy/Astrophysics

Astronomical Journal
Astronomy
Astronomy and Astrophysics
Astrophysical Journal
Earth and Planetary Science Letters
Icarus
Mercury
Planetary and Space Science
Royal Astronomical Society. Monthly Notices
Sky and Telescope

Biochemistry and Biophysics

Analytical Biochemistry
Archives of Biochemistry and Biophysics
Biochemical and Biophysical Research Communications
Biochemical Journal
Biochemistry (U.S.)
Biochimica et Biophysica Acta
European Journal of Biochemistry
FEBS Letters, Federation of European Biochemical Societies
Journal of Biological Chemistry
Journal of Cell Biology
Journal of Molecular Biology

Biology

Applied and Environmental Microbiology
Biological Bulletin
Biological Reviews of the Cambridge Philosophical Society
Bioscience
Brain Research
Chromosoma
Developmental Biology
Ecology

Evolution
Experimental Cell Research
FEBS Letters, Federation of European Biochemical Societies
Federation of American Societies for Experimental Biology.
    Proceedings
Genetics
Journal of Anatomy
Journal of Applied Physiology
Journal of Bacteriology
Journal of Ecology
Journal of Experimental Biology
Journal of General Physiology
Journal of Molecular Biology
Journal of Physiology
Journal of Ultrastructure Research
Proceedings of the Royal Society. Series B. Biological
    Sciences
Quarterly Review of Biology
Society for Experimental Biology and Medicine. Proceedings
Virology

Botany

American Journal of Botany
Annals of Botany
Botanical Gazette
Botanical Review
Canadian Journal of Botany
Economic Botany
Journal of Experimental Botany
Phytopathology
Plant Physiology
Torrey Botanical Club. Bulletin

Chemistry

American Chemical Society. Journal
Analytical Chemistry

Angewandte Chemie
Chemical Physics Letters
Chemical Society, London.   Journal
Chemische Berichte
Inorganic Chemistry
Journal of Chemical Physics
Journal of Organic Chemistry
Tetrahedron
Tetrahedron Letters

Engineering

American Society of Civil Engineers.   Proceedings
Bell System Technical Journal
Civil Engineering
Consulting Engineer
Electronics
Engineer
Engineering (London)
Engineering Journal
Engineering News Record
Franklin Institute, Philadelphia.   Journal
IEEE Spectrum
International Journal of Engineering Science
Journal of Mechanical Design.   Transactions of the A.S.M.E.
Professional Engineer
Society of Engineers.   Journal
Technology Review
Trend in Engineering

General Science

American Journal of Science
American Scientist
Comptes Rendus des Sciences de l'Academie des Sciences
Experientia
Nature

New Scientist
Royal Society of London.   Proceedings
Science
Scientific American

Geology

American Association of Petroleum Geologists.   Bulletin
Earth and Planetary Science Letters
Geological Society of America.   Bulletin
Geology
Geotimes
Journal of Geophysical Research

Mathematics

American Mathematical Monthly
American Mathematical Society.   Bulletin
SIAM News
SIAM Review

Medicine

American Journal of Cardiology
American Journal of Medicine
American Journal of Public Health
American Medical Association.   Journal
British Medical Journal
Cancer Research
Infection and Immunity
Journal of Clinical Endocrinology and Metabolism
Journal of Clinical Investigation
Journal of Experimental Medicine
Journal of Immunology
Journal of Pediatrics
Journal of Pharmacology and Experimental Therapeutics
Lancet

New England Journal of Medicine
World Health Organization Chronicle

Physics

Journal of Applied Physics
Physical Review
Physical Review Letters
Physics Letters
Reviews of Modern Physics

Zoology

American Naturalist
American Zoologist
Animal Behaviour
Canadian Journal of Zoology
Condor
Copeia
Journal of Economic Entomology
Journal of Experimental Zoology
Journal of Mammalogy
Journal of Zoology
Natural History
Physiological Entomology
Physiological Zoology
Systematic Entomology

Appendix III
Databases and Their Sources

There are well over 100 databases in science, technology, and agriculture. These databases are given in the following chart and are organized by subject. Also included in the chart is the index to which the database corresponds and/or the sponsoring agency which produces the database. The five vendors selling the database services are DIALOG Information Retrieval Service (DIALOG) located in Palo Alto, California; Systems Development Corporation (SDC) located in Santa Monica, California; Bibliographic Retrieval Services, Inc. (BRS) located in Scotia, New York; the National Library of Medicine (NLM) located in Bethesda, Maryland; and Institute for Scientific Information (ISI) located in Philadelphia, Pennsylvania. Beneath the name of each vendor is the beginning date of the coverage of the database. Comments are included where needed.

Agriculture

Database	Index and/or Sponsor	Service and Coverage	Comments
AGLINE	(Doane Information Center Indexing Service)	ORBIT 1977–	
AGRICOLA	Bibliography of Agriculture (National Agricultural Library)	DIALOG 1970– BRS 1970–	
AQUACULTURE	(National Oceanic and Atmospheric Administration)	DIALOG 1970–	
CAB ABSTRACTS	26 abstract titles published by the Commonwealth Agricultural Bureaux	DIALOG 1973–	
CRIS/USDA	(U.S. Department of Agriculture)	DIALOG July 1974–	
DICIS	(Doane Agricultural Services, Inc.)	ORBIT SDC 1972–	
FOOD SCIENCE AND TECHNOLOGY ABSTRACTS or FSTA	Food Science and Technology Abstracts (International Food Information Service)	DIALOG 1969– ORBIT 1969–	
FOODS ADLIBRA	(Komp Information Services)	DIALOG 1974–	
PESTDOC/ PESTDOC-II	PESTDOC Abstract Journal (Derwent Publications, Ltd.)	ORBIT 1950's–	

Database	Index and/or Sponsor	Service and Coverage	Comments
RANGE	U.S.-Canadian Range Management (The Oryx Press)	ORBIT 1935-	
TROPAG	Abstracts on Tropical Agriculture (Royal Tropical Institute of Amsterdam)	ORBIT 1975-	
VETDOC	VETDOC Abstract Journal (Derwent Publications, Ltd.)	ORBIT 1968-	

Biology

Database	Index and/or Sponsor	Service and Coverage	Comments
AQUATIC SCIENCES AND FISHERIES ABSTRACTS	Aquatic Sciences and Fisheries Abstracts (NOAA/Cambridge Scientific Abstracts)	DIALOG 1978-	
BIOCODES	BIOSIS Search Guide (Biosciences Information Service)	ORBIT 1969-	Covers category codes, taxonomic codes, and their full names and cross references
BIOSIS PREVIEWS and BIOSIS/ BIO7479/BIO6973	Biological Abstracts and Biological Abstracts/RRM (formerly Bioresearch Index) (Biosciences Information Service)	DIALOG 1969- ORBIT 1969- BRS 1970-	
LIFE SCIENCE COLLECTION	(Cambridge Scientific Abstracts)	DIALOG 1978-	

Database	Index and/or Sponsor	Service and Coverage	Comments
Pacific Island Ecosystems (PIE)	(Office of Biological Services of the U.S. Fish and Wildlife Service)	ORBIT 1927-	
ZOOLOGICAL RECORD	Zoological Record (Bio Science Information Service)	DIALOG 1978-	

Chemistry

Database	Index and/or Sponsor	Service and Coverage	Comments
CA-CONDENSATES	Chemical Abstracts Condensates (Chemical Abstracts Service)	BRS 1970-76	
CA SEARCH	Chemical Abstracts (Chemical Abstracts Service)	DIALOG 1967- / BRS 1977-	
CAS 67 CAS 72 CAS 77 CAS 82 CHEMSDI	Chemical Abstracts (Chemical Abstracts Service)	DIALOG / ORBIT 1967-71 1972-76 1977-81 1982-	
CHEMDEX/ CHEMDEX2/ CHEMDEX3	Chemical Abstracts (Chemical Abstracts Service)	ORBIT 1972-	Chemical dictionary for Chemical Abstracts
CHEMICAL REGULATIONS AND GUIDELINES SYSTEM (CRGS)	Federal Register (U.S. Interagency Regulatory Liaison Group)	DIALOG	
CHEMLINE	Chemicals identified by Chemical Abstracts Service (National Library of Medicine)	NLM	Chemical dictionary

Database	Index and/or Sponsor	Service and Coverage		Comments
CHEMNAME[TM]	(DIALOG Information Retrieval Service and Chemical Abstracts Service)	DIALOG		Chemical name dictionary
CHEMSEARCH[TM]	(DIALOG Information Retrieval Service and Chemical Abstracts Service)	DIALOG		
CHEMSIS[TM]	(DIALOG Information Retrieval Service and Chemical Abstracts Service)	DIALOG 1967–		
CIN (CHEMICAL INDUSTRY NOTES)	Chemical Industry Notes (Chemical Abstracts Service)	DIALOG 1974–	ORBIT 1974–	
CLAIMS[TM]/CHEM	Includes Chemical Abstracts (Abstract number) and Official Gazette (IFI/ Plenum Data Co.)	DIALOG 1950–1962		
CLAIMS[TM]/UNITERM	(IFI/Plenum Co.)	DIALOG 1950–		
CRDS (Chemical Reactions Documentation Service)	Journal of Synthetic Methods (Derwent Publications, Ltd.)		ORBIT 1944–	

Engineering and Technology

Database	Index and/or Sponsor	Service and Coverage	Comments
APILIT	(American Petroleum Institute)	ORBIT 1964–	Petroleum literature, especially refining and petrochemical industry
APIPAT	(American Petroleum Institute)	ORBIT 1964–	Refining patents
AQUALINE	(Water Research Centre)	DIALOG 1974–	
BHRA FLUID ENGINEERING	(British Hydromechanics Research Association)	DIALOG 1974–	
CLAIMS^{TM}/CITATION	(Search Check, Inc., and IFI/Plenum Data Co.)	DIALOG 1947–1981	Designed to answer questions when later patents cite another patent
CLAIMS^{TM}/CLASS	(IFI/Plenum Data Co.)	DIALOG	Classification code and title dictionary
CLAIMS^{TM}/U.S. PATENTS	Official Gazette (IFI/Plenum Data Co.)	DIALOG 1963–1970	
CLAIMS^{TM}/U.S. PATENT ABSTRACTS	(IFI/Plenum Data Co.)	DIALOG 1971–	
CLAIMS^{TM}/U.S. PATENT ABSTRACTS WEEKLY	(IFI/Plenum Data Co.)	DIALOG Current month	

Database	Index and/or Sponsor	Service and Coverage			Comments
COMPENDEX	Engineering Index Monthly (Engineering Information, Inc.)	DIALOG 1970–	ORBIT 1970–	BRS 1976–	
DOE ENERGY	(U.S. Department of Energy)	DIALOG 1974–			
EBIB	Energy Bibliography & Index (Gulf Publishing Co.)		ORBIT 1919–		
EDB	(U.S. Department of Energy)		ORBIT 1974–		
ENERGYLINE[R]	Energy Information Abstracts and Environment Abstracts (Environment Information Center, Inc.)	DIALOG 1971–	ORBIT 1971–	BRS 1971–	
ENERGYNET	(Environment Information Center, Inc.)	DIALOG Current Information			
EPIA	INFORUM (Edison Electric Institute)		ORBIT 1975–		Environmental aspects of new power plants & related facilities e.g. electric, solar, nuclear, coal, gas, geothermal, hydro-electric
FEDERAL ENERGY DATA INDEX	EIA Publications Directory, EIA Data Index			BRS 1977–	

Database	Index and/or Sponsor	Service and Coverage	Comments
INPADOC	(International Patent Document Center)	DIALOG Most recent 6 weeks	
INSPEC (see Science and Technology)			
ISMEC	(Cambridge Scientific Abstracts)	DIALOG 1973-	
METADEX (METALS ABSTRACTS/ ALLOYS INDEX)	Metals Abstracts and Alloys Index (American Society for Metals)	DIALOG 1966- (Alloys Index, 1974-)	
NONFERROUS METALS ABSTRACTS	Nonferrous Metals Abstracts (British Nonferrous Metals Technology Center)	DIALOG 1961-	
P/E NEWS	(American Petroleum Institute)	ORBIT 1975-	
PIRA	Paper & Board Abstracts, Printing Abstracts, Packaging Abstracts, and Management and Marketing Abstracts (Research Association for the Paper and Board Printing and Packaging Industries)	DIALOG 1975-	
POWER	(Energy Library. U.S. Department of Energy)	ORBIT 1950's	

Database	Index and/or Sponsor	Service and Coverage	Comments
RAPRA ABSTRACTS	Rubber and Plastics Research Abstracts (Rubber and Plastics Research Association of Great Britain)	DIALOG 1972–	
SAE	SAE Abstracts (Society of Automotive Engineers, Inc.)	ORBIT 1965–	
SURFACE COATING ABSTRACTS	(Paint Research Association of Great Britain)	DIALOG 1976–	
SWRA	Selected Water Resources Abstracts (Water Resources Scientific Information Center)	ORBIT 1968–	
TITUS	(Institut Textile de France)	ORBIT 1967–	World textile literature
TRIS (Transportation Research Service)	(U.S. Department of Transportation Research Board)	DIALOG 1968–	
TULSA	Petroleum Abstracts (University of Tulsa, Information Service Department)	ORBIT 1965–	
WATERLIT	(South African Water Information Centre)	ORBIT 1976–	World-wide water resources and literature
WELDASEARCH	(Welding Institute)	DIALOG 1967–	

Database	Index and/or Sponsor	Service and Coverage			Comments
WORLD ALUMINUM ABSTRACTS	(American Society for Metals)	DIALOG 1968-			
WORLD TEXTILES	World Textile Abstracts (Shirley Institute)	DIALOG 1970-			
Environment					
ENVIROLINE^R	Environment Abstracts (Environment Information Center, Inc.)	DIALOG 1971-	ORBIT 1971-	BRS 1971-	
ENVIRONMENTAL BIBLIOGRAPHY	Environmental Periodicals Bibliography (Environmental Studies Institute)	DIALOG 1973-			
ENVIRONMENTAL IMPACT STATEMENTS	(Information Resource Press)			BRS 1977-	
IRIS	(U.S. Environmental Protection Agency Information Project)	DIALOG 1979-			
TSCA INITIAL INVENTORY	(U.S. Environmental Protection Agency, DIALOG Information Retrieval Service)	DIALOG 1979			

Geology

Database	Index and/or Sponsor	Service and Coverage			Comments
GEOARCHIVE	Geotitles Weekly, Geocom Bulletin, Geoscience Documentation and Bibliography of Vertebrate Paleontology (Geosystems)	DIALOG 1969-			
GEOREF or GeoRef	Bibliography and Index of Geology and more (American Geological Institute)	DIALOG 1961-	ORBIT 1961-		
ISI/ GeoSciTech	GeoSciTech Citation Index and Current Contents. GeoSciTech (Institute for Scientific Information)	ISI 1978-			

Government Documents, United States

Database	Index and/or Sponsor	Service and Coverage			Comments
ASI	American Statistics Index (Congressional Information Service)	DIALOG 1973-			
CIS	Index to Publications of the United States Congress (Congressional Information Service)	DIALOG 1970-			
GPO MONTHLY CATALOG	Monthly Catalog of U.S. Government Publications (U.S. Government Printing Office)	DIALOG 1976-	ORBIT 1976-	BRS 1976-	

Mathematics

Database	Index and/or Sponsor	Service and Coverage	Comments
ISI/CompuMath™	CompuMath Citation Index™	ISI 1976–	
MATHFILE	Mathematical Reviews	DIALOG 1973–	

Medicine

Database	Index and/or Sponsor	Service and Coverage	Comments
AVLINE	National Library of Medicine Audiovisuals Catalog, NLM Current Catalog Proof Sheets, Health Sciences Audiovisuals, National Medical Audiovisual Center Catalog (National Library of Medicine)	NLM Audiovisuals cataloged by NLM since 1975	
BIOETHICS	Bibliography of Bioethics (Kennedy Institute of Ethics)	NLM 1973–	Covers value questions in health
CANCERLIT	Cancer Therapy Abstracts, Carcinogenesis Abstracts (National Cancer Institute)	NLM 1963–	Covers all aspects of cancer
CANCERPROJ	(National Cancer Institute)	NLM Current investigations	Summaries of on-going cancer research projects

Database	Index and/or Sponsor	Service and Coverage	Comments
CLINPROT	(National Cancer Institute)	NLM Current investigations	Summaries of research on new anti-cancer agents
EPILEPSY	Epilepsy Abstracts (National Institute of Neurological and Communicative Disorders and Stroke)	NLM 1945–	
EXCERPTA MEDICA	(Excerpta Medica)	DIALOG 1974–	
HEALTH PLANNING & ADMINISTRATION	Hospital Literature Index, et al.	DIALOG 1975– NLM 1975– BRS 1975–	Non-clinical aspects of health care delivery
HISTLINE	Bibliography of the History of Medicine	NLM 1970–	
INTERNATIONAL PHARMACEUTICAL ABSTRACTS	International Pharmaceutical Abstracts (American Society of Hospital Pharmacists)	DIALOG 1970–	
ISI/BIOMED	(Institute for Scientific Information)	ISI 1979–	Biomedical literature from Science Citation Index
MEDLINE and BACKFILES	Index Medicus, International Nursing Index, Index to Dental Literature	DIALOG 1966– NLM 1966– BRS 1966–	
MEDOC	(Eccles Health Science Library, Univ. of Utah)	BRS 1975–	Government documents in health sciences

Database	Index and/or Sponsor	Service and Coverage	Comments
RINGDOC/ RING6475	RINGDOC Abstract Journal	ORBIT 1964–	Pharmaceutical literature
RTECS	Registry of Toxic Effects of Chemical Substances (National Institute for Occupational Safety and Health)	NLM	Toxic dose information
TOXLINE and TOXBACK	Chemical-Biological Activities, Abstracts on Health Effects of Environmental Pollutants, International Pharmaceutical Abstracts, Toxicity Bibliography, Pesticides Abstracts, Hayes File, et al.	NLM 1965–	Toxicological literature
TDB	(National Library of Medicine)	NLM	Detailed information on the most important toxic substances

Physics

Database	Index and/or Sponsor	Service and Coverage	Comments
METEOROLOGICAL AND GEOASTRO- PHYSICAL ABSTRACTS	Meteorological and Geoastro- physical Abstracts (American Meteorological Society and NOAA)	DIALOG 1972–	
SPIN	(American Institute of Physics)	DIALOG 1975–	

Pollution

Database	Index and/or Sponsor	Service and Coverage	Comments
APTIC	Includes Air Pollution Abstracts (Manpower and Technical Information Branch, U.S. Environmental Protection Agency)	DIALOG 1966- September 1978	
POLLUTION ABSTRACTS	Pollution Abstracts (Cambridge Scientific Abstracts)	DIALOG 1970- BRS 1970-	

Science and Technology

Database	Index and/or Sponsor	Service and Coverage	Comments
COLD REGIONS	Antarctic Bibliography and Bibliography on Cold Regions Science and Technology (U.S. Army Corps of Engineers)	ORBIT 1962-	
CONFERENCE PAPERS INDEX	Conference Papers Index (Xerox University Microfilm)	DIALOG 1973-	
ELCOM	Electronics & Communications Abstracts Journal and Computer & Information Systems Abstracts Journal	ORBIT 1977-	
FOREST	(Forest Products Research Society)	ORBIT 1947-	

Database	Index and/or Sponsor	Service and Coverage			Comments
		DIALOG	ORBIT	BRS	
INSPEC or INSPEC/INSP6976	Physics Abstracts, Electrical and Electronics Abstracts and Computer and Control Abstracts (Institution of Electrical Engineers)	DIALOG 1969–	ORBIT 1969–	BRS 1969–	
NTIS or NTIS/NTIS6469	Weekly Government Abstracts and Government Report Announcements (National Technical Information Service)	DIALOG 1964–	ORBIT 1964–	BRS 1970–	
OCEANIC ABSTRACTS or OCEANIC	Oceanic Abstracts (Cambridge Scientific Abstracts)	DIALOG 1964–			
PAPERCHEM	Abstract Bulletin of the Institute of Paper Chemistry (Institute of Paper Chemistry)		ORBIT 1969–		
SAFETY	Safety Science Abstracts Journal (Cambridge Scientific Abstracts, Inc.)		ORBIT 1975–		

Science, Technology and Agriculture

Database	Index and/or Sponsor	Service and Coverage			Comments
COMPREHENSIVE DISSERTATION INDEX or DISSERTATION ABSTRACTS	Comprehensive Dissertation Index, Dissertation Abstracts International, and American Doctoral Dissertations (Xerox University Microfilms)	DIALOG 1861–		BRS 1861–	

Database	Index and/or Sponsor	Service and Coverage		Comments
DATABASE INDEX		ORBIT		Online index to all ORBIT databases
INTERNATIONAL SOFTWARE DIRECTORY	International Software Directory (Imprint Editions)	DIALOG		
ISI/ISTP&B[TM]	Index to Scientific and Technical Proceedings (Institute for Scientific Information)		ISI 1978–	
MAGAZINE INDEX	Magazine Index (Information Access Corporation)	DIALOG 1976–		
MICROCOMPUTER INDEX[TM]	Microcomputer Index (Microcomputer Information Services)	DIALOG 1980–		
PATSEARCH	Official Gazette (Superintendent of Documents)		BRS 1971–	
SCISEARCH[R]	Science Citation Index and Current Contents (Institute for Scientific Information)	DIALOG 1965–	ORBIT 1977–	
SSIE CURRENT RESEARCH or SSIE	(Smithsonian Science Information Exchange, Inc.)	DIALOG last two years	ORBIT 1978–	BRS 1977–

Database	Index and/or Sponsor	Service and Coverage	Comments
US PATENTS or USPA/USP77/USP70	(Pergamon International Information Corporation)	ORBIT 1971– BRS 1860–	
WPI/WPIL	Central Patents Index and World Patent Index (Derwent Publications, Ltd.)	ORBIT varies from 1963–	

Appendix IV
A Selected List of Sources for Review Articles

General Science

Annual Review of Information Science and Technology. Chicago:
Encyclopaedia Britannica, 1966--

Endeavour. Elmsford, N.Y.: Pergamon Press, 1948--

Science Progress. Oxford, England: Blackwell Scientific
Publications, 1894--

Agriculture

Advances in Agronomy. New York: Academic Press, 1949--

Advances in Food Research. New York: Academic Press, 1948--

Advances in Veterinary Sciences. New York: Academic Press,
1953--

CRC Critical Reviews in Food Science and Nutrition.
Boca Raton, Fla.: Chemical Rubber Company, 1970--

CRC Critical Reviews in Plant Sciences. Boca Raton, Fla.:
Chemical Rubber Company, 1983--

Biology

Advances in Applied Microbiology. New York: Academic
Press, 1959--

Advances in Biological and Medical Physics. New York:
Academic Press, 1948--

Advances in Botanical Research. New York: Academic Press,
1963--

Advances in Comparative Physiology and Biochemistry.
New York: Academic Press, 1962--

Advances in Ecological Research.   New York: Academic Press,
1962--

Advances in Enzyme Regulation.   New York: Pergamon Press,
1963--

Advances in Genetics.   New York: Academic Press, 1907--

Advances in Human Genetics.   New York: Plenum, 1970--

Advances in Insect Physiology.   New York: Academic Press,
1963--

Advances in Marine Biology.   New York: Academic Press,
1963--

Advances in Microbiology of the Sea.   New York: Academic
Press, 1968--

Advances in Parasitology.   New York: Academic Press, 1963--

Advances in Study of Behavior.   New York: Academic Press,
1965--

Advances in Virus Research.   New York: Academic Press, 1953--

Annual Review of Ecology and Systematics.   Palo Alto, Calif.:
Annual Reviews, Inc., 1970--

Annual Review of Entomology.   Palo Alto, Calif.:   Annual
Reviews, Inc., 1956--

Annual Review of Genetics.   Palo Alto, Calif.:   Annual
Reviews, Inc., 1967--

Annual Review of Microbiology.   Palo Alto, Calif.:   Annual
Reviews, Inc., 1947--

Annual Review of Physiology.   Palo Alto, Calif.:   Annual
Reviews, Inc., 1950--

Annual Review of Phytopathology.   Palo Alto, Calif.:   Annual
Reviews, Inc., 1963--

Annual Review of Plant Physiology.   New York: Academic
Press, 1950--

Biological Reviews of the Cambridge Philosophical Society.
Cambridge, England: Cambridge University Press, 1923--

Botanical Review.   Bronx, N.Y.:   New York Botanical Garden,
1935--

CRC Critical Reviews in Clinical Laboratory Sciences.
    Boca Raton, Fla.:   Chemical Rubber Company, 1970--

CRC Critical Reviews in Microbiology.   Boca Raton, Fla.:
    Chemical Rubber Company, 1971--

CRC Critical Reviews in Plant Sciences.   Boca Raton, Fla.:
    Chemical Rubber Company, 1983--

CRC Critical Reviews in Toxicology.   Boca Raton, Fla.:
    Chemical Rubber Company, 1971--

Current Advances in Ecological Sciences.   New York:
    Pergamon Press, 1975--

Current Topics in Developmental Biology.   New York: Academic
    Press, 1966--

Current Topics in Bioenergetics.   New York: Academic Press,
    1966--

Evolutionary Biology.   New York: Appleton, 1967--

International Review of Cytology.   New York: Academic Press,
    1952--

Microbiological Reviews.   Washington: American Society for
    Microbiology, 1937--

Oceanography and Marine Biology, An Annual Review.   Aberdeen,
    Scotland: Aberdeen University Press, 1963--

Physiological Reviews.   Bethesda, Md.:   American Physiological
    Society, 1921--

Progress in Theoretical Biology.   New York: Academic Press,
    1967--

Progress in Nucleic Acid Research and Molecular Biology.
    New York: Academic Press, 1963--

The Quarterly Review of Biology.   Stony Brook, N.Y.:   Stony
    Brook Foundation, State University of New York, 1926--

Recent Progress in Hormone Research.   Proceedings of the
    Laurentian Hormone Conference.   New York: Academic
    Press, 1947--

Vitamins and Hormones: Advances in Research and Applications.
    New York: Academic Press, 1943--

Chemistry

Advances in Biochemical Psychopharmacology.   New York:
    Raven Press, 1969--

Advances in Chemistry Series. Washington: American Chemical
    Society, 1950--

Advances in Heterocyclic Chemistry. New York: Academic
    Press, 1963--

Advances in Inorganic Chemistry and Radiochemistry. New York:
    Academic Press, 1959--

Advances in Macromolecular Chemistry. New York: Academic
    Press, 1968--

Advances in Organic Chemistry. New York: Wiley (Inter-
    science), 1960--

Advances in Organometallic Chemistry. New York: Academic
    Press, 1964--

Advances in Photochemistry. New York: Wiley, 1963--

Advances in Physical Organic Chemistry. New York: Academic
    Press, 1963--

Advances in Polymer Science. New York: Springer-Verlag,
    1958--

Advances in Quantum Chemistry. New York: Academic Press,
    1964--

Annual Reports in Medicinal Chemistry. American Chemical
    Society. New York: Academic Press, 1965--

Annual Review of Biochemistry. Stanford, Calif.: Stanford
    University Press, 1932--

Annual Review of Physical Chemistry. Palo Alto, Calif.:
    Annual Reviews, Inc., 1950--

Chemical Reviews. Washington: American Chemical Society,
    1924--

Chemical Society Reviews. London: Chemical Society, 1972--

Chemical Zoology. New York: Academic Press, 1967--

Chemistry and Physics of Carbon; a Series of Advances.
    New York: M. Dekker, 1966--

CRC Critical Reviews in Analytical Chemistry. Boca Raton,
    Fla.: Chemical Rubber Company, 1970--

CRC Critical Reviews in Biochemistry. Boca Raton, Fla.:
    Chemical Rubber Company, 1972--

Electroanalytical Chemistry; a Series of Advances. New York:
    M. Dekker, 1966--

Macromolecular Reviews. New York: Wiley, 1967--

Progress in Inorganic Chemistry. New York: Wiley
    (Interscience), 1959--

Progress in Solid State Chemistry. Elmsford, N.Y.:
    Pergamon, 1964--

Survey of Progress in Chemistry. New York: Academic Press,
    1963--

Transition Metal Chemistry; a Series of Advances. New York:
    M. Dekker, 1965--

Engineering

Advances in Applied Mechanics. New York: Academic Press,
    1948-- Supplements, 1961--

Advances in Chemical Engineering. New York: Academic Press,
    1948--

Advances in Cryogenic Engineering. New York: Plenum, 1960--

Advances in Electrochemistry and Electrochemical Engineering.
    New York: Wiley (Interscience), 1961--

Advances in Electronics and Electron Physics. New York:
    Academic Press, 1948--

Advances in Environmental Science and Technology. New York:
    Wiley (Interscience), 1969--

Advances in Heat Transfer. New York: Academic Press, 1964--

Advances in Information Systems Science. New York: Plenum,
    1969--

Advances in Water Pollution Research. Elmsford, N.Y.:
    Pergamon Press, 1962--

Annual Review of Energy. Palo Alto, Calif.: Annual Reviews,
    Inc., 1976--

Applied Mechanics Review. New York: American Society of
    Mechanical Engineers, 1948--

Biotechnology and Bioengineering. New York: Wiley
    (Interscience), 1958--

CRC Critical Reviews in Biomedical Engineering. Boca Raton,
    Fla.: Chemical Rubber Company, 1971--

CRC Critical Reviews in Environmental Control. Boca Raton,
    Fla.: Chemical Rubber Company, 1970--

CRC Critical Reviews in Solid State Sciences and Material
    Sciences. Boca Raton, Fla.: Chemical Rubber Company,
    1970--

Progress in Astronautics and Aeronautics Series. New York:
    Academic Press, 1968--

Reviews in Engineering Geology. Boulder, Colo.: Geological
    Society of America, 1961--

Geology

Advances in Environmental Sciences. New York: Wiley
    (Interscience), 1969--

Advances in Geophysics. New York: Academic Press, 1952--

Advances in Hydroscience. New York: Academic Press, 1964--

Advances in Organic Geochemistry. New York: Pergamon Press,
    1956--

Progress in Oceanography. Elmsford, N.Y.: Pergamon Press,
    1963--

Medicine

Advances in Clinical Chemistry. New York: Academic Press,
    1958--

Advances in Immunology. New York: Academic Press, 1961--

Advances in Internal Medicine. Chicago: Year Book Medical
    Pub., 1942--

Advances in Pharmacology and Chemotherapy. New York:
    Academic Press, 1962--

Advances in Surgery. Chicago: Year Book Medical Pub.,
    1965--

Annual Review of Medicine: Selected Topics in Clinical
    Sciences. Palo Alto, Calif.: Annual Reviews, Inc.,
    1950--

Annual Review of Pharmacology and Toxicology. Palo Alto,
    Calif.: Annual Reviews, Inc., 1961--

CRC Critical Reviews in Biomedical Engineering. Boca Raton,
    Fla.: Chemical Rubber Company, 1971--

CRC Critical Reviews in Clinical Laboratory Sciences.
    Boca Raton, Fla.: Chemical Rubber Company, 1970--

CRC Critical Reviews in Diagnostic Imaging. Boca Raton, Fla.:
    Chemical Rubber Company, 1970--

CRC Critical Reviews in Immunology. Boca Raton, Fla.:
    Chemical Rubber Company, 1979--

CRC Critical Reviews in Toxicology. Boca Raton, Fla.:
    Chemical Rubber Company, 1971--

International Review of Experimental Pathology. New York:
    Academic Press, 1962--

Methods in Cancer Research. New York: Academic Press, 1967--

Pathology Annual. New York: Appleton-Century-Crofts, 1966--

Pharmacological Reviews. American Society for Pharmacology
    and Experimental Therapeutics. Baltimore: Williams &
    Wilkins, 1951--

Physiological Reviews. Bethesda, Md.: American Physiological
    Society, 1921--

Progress in Clinical Cancer. New York: Grune & Stratton,
    1965--

Progress in Clinical Pathology. New York: Grune & Stratton,
    1966--

Progress in Experimental Tumor Research. Basel, Switzerland:
    Karger, 1960--

Progress in Medical Virology. Basil, Switzerland:
    Karger, 1958--

Progress in Neurological Surgery. Basil, Switzerland:
    Karger, 1966--

Progress in Surgery. Basil, Switzerland: Karger, 1961--

                            Nutrition

Annual Review of Nutrition. Palo Alto, Calif.: Annual
    Reviews, Inc., 1981--

CRC Critical Reviews in Food Science and Nutrition. Boca
    Raton, Fla.: Chemical Rubber Company, 1970--

World Review of Nutrition and Dietetics. Basel, Switzerland:
    Karger, 1964--

Physics

Advances in Atomic and Molecular Physics. New York:
    Academic Press, 1965--

Advances in Chemical Physics. New York: Wiley (Interscience)
    1958--

Advances in Chromatography. New York: M. Dekker, 1965--

Advances in Electronics and Electron Physics. New York:
    Academic Press, 1948-- Supplements, 1963--

Advances in Magnetic Resonance. New York: Academic Press,
    1965--

Advances in Nuclear Physics. New York: Plenum Press, 1968--

Annual Review of Nuclear and Particle Science. Palo Alto,
    Calif.: Annual Reviews, Inc., 1952--

Applied Spectroscopy Reviews. New York: M. Dekker, 1967--

Progress in Nuclear Energy. Elmsford, N.Y.: Pergamon,
    1956-- (Published in 12 series at irregular intervals.)

Reviews of Plasma Physics. New York: Plenum, 1965--

Solid State Physics: Advances in Research and Applications.
    New York: Academic Press, 1955-- Supplements, 1958--

Index

Journals, 9, 10, 11, 12, 13, 14, 33, 133-138
  agriculture, 133
  astronomy, 134
  astrophysics, 134
  biochemistry, 134
  biology, 134-135
  biophysics, 134
  botany, 135
  chemistry, 135-136
  engineering, 136
  general science, 136-137
  geology, 137
  mathematics, 137
  medicine, 137-138
  physics, 138
  zoology, 138
Journals, scientific, 1-2
Journals, trade, 2

Library of Congress Subject Headings, 18-19
Literature cited, 124-128
  how to cite government documents, 127-128
  how to cite the literature, 124-125
Logic, computer, 101-103

Magazine Index, 27, 33-34
  database, 33
  procedure for using, 34
MAGAZINE INDEX database, 34, 155
Manuals
  see handbook
Mathematical Reviews, 30, 53-55
  database, 53, 150
  order of search, 53
  procedure for using, 54-55
Mathematics
  abstracts and indexes, 53-55
  journals, 137
MATHFILE database, 53, 150
Medicine
  abstracts and indexes, 30, 55-59, 64-65, 131-132
  databases, 55, 58, 110-111, 150-152
  journals, 137-138
  review sources, 162-163
MEDLINE database, 55, 97, 103, 110-111, 151
Microcatalogs
  see card catalog
Monthly Catalog to U.S. Government Publications, 27, 81-83, 85
  cumulative, 84
  database, 149
  order of search, 82
  procedure for using, 82-83

About the Authors

EILEEN PRITCHARD is Science Librarian and Coordinator of Automated Retrieval at California Polytechnic State University, San Luis Obispo. Her articles have appeared in *Journal of Technical Writing and Communication* and the *Canadian Journal of Genetics and Cytology*.

PAULA R. SCOTT is Curriculum Cataloger at California Polytechnic State University. Her articles have appeared in *California Librarian* and in the anthology *International Agricultural Librarianship*.